Come to the Feast

a companion to
Common Worship
Holy Communion

Gill Ambrose
Simon Kershaw

Canterbury Press
Norwich

First published in 2001 by The Canterbury Press Norwich
(a publishing imprint of Hymns Ancient & Modern Limited,
a registered charity)
St Mary's Works, St Mary's Plain,
Norwich, Norfolk, NR3 3BH.

A catalogue record for this book
is available from the British Library

ISBN 1-85311-450-2

Designed and typeset by crucix www.crucix.com
in Joanna and Gill Sans, with Golden Cockerel for display

Printed in Great Britain by Creative Print & Design (Wales)

Contents

Preface: How to Use This Book

Come to the Feast is a companion to the service of Holy Communion in *Common Worship*. It aims to help develop and nourish the faith of worshippers by exploring and explaining the words and actions of the Eucharist.

At the heart of the book is the text of Order One, the most commonly used form of the service of Holy Communion in the Church of England. You can use this in church as a service book, and the short comments which accompany it are intended to help focus thoughts and prayers as you worship.

You can also use *Come to the Feast* out of church. The commentary can be used to direct preparation for the service and to suggest further areas of thought and study. The Bible references can be explored to see the wider context from which many of the words of the service are taken.

The other chapters of the book explore several topics in greater depth. Each of these chapters is intended to stand on its own, and you can read each of them as you want to find out more about a particular area. They cover subjects such as the history of the Eucharist, the diverse ways in which the Eucharist is celebrated, the shape of the service, and under-standing parts of the service such as the creed and the eucharistic prayers. These chapters can also be used as part of a study course on the Eucharist. At the end there are suggestions for further reading in a number of areas, and a short glossary.

The Eucharist is central to our lives as Christians. We hope that this book will help each of us appreciate better the saving grace made present to us by Jesus Christ, the bread of life.

Introduction: Come to the Feast

Each week Christians around the world gather in groups, small, medium and large, to celebrate the Eucharist together. The Eucharist is the central act of worship of Christians, and over the last century or so it has increasingly been the usual Sunday morning service in churches across the Church of England: 'the Lord's own service for the Lord's own people on the Lord's own day'.

The introduction of *Common Worship* prompted a flurry of books for clergy, worship leaders and students of the liturgy. *Come to the Feast*, however, is intended for worshippers who want to learn something about the service in which we take part. As the subtitle indicates, it is a companion to the service; and it is appropriate, perhaps, that the word 'companion' originally meant someone with whom we share bread.

The General Notes, which are found at the beginning of the eucharistic texts in *Common Worship*, remind us that 'careful devotional preparation is recommended for every communicant', and the book provides several forms of prayer which are suitable for this. The Notes go on to tell us that Holy Communion is celebrated by the whole community gathered for worship and that the ministry of members of the congregation is expressed through their participation in the service in many and varied ways.

We hope that this small book will help worshippers both to prepare for and to participate in the service. For those who are unfamiliar with the Eucharist, we hope that both the commentary on the words and actions, and the short chapters which follow, will provide explanations to help you under-stand why things happen as they do, so that you can participate more knowledgeably. For those who have been communicants for longer, we hope that the opportunity to learn again about the service, and something of the tradition which formed it, will bring new insights and perhaps enable better preparation beforehand.

The way in which we prepare to take part in the service and receive communion will be different for each of us and will depend on our circumstances, our tradition and our personality. This is right and good. Some will have the time for study and prayer which can only be a dream for, say, a parent with several small children who has almost no time alone. And while some will find it easy to concentrate in a focused way when they take part in the service, others will experience considerable distraction, or an over-familiarity which means that the words are said but the attention wanders. The explanations alongside the text are intended to help us to be more aware of the form and structure of the Eucharist. As we travel through the service, whatever the distractions, we will be more confident of the way we are going and more observant on the journey.

In this book, then, we place first and foremost the words of the service itself. Taken from Order One of *Common Worship*, this is the service most of the Church of England will be familiar with. Alongside it are explanatory comments, Bible references, suggestions for further investigation and pointers to topics discussed elsewhere.

After this, we look at the history and context of the Eucharist, at the basic structure of the service, and how both the content and the style of celebration may be varied from a simple and brief said service to a lengthy service with music and singing, and lots of elaboration. We explain the rhythm and history of the year – its highpoints at Easter and Christmas, the space we are afforded by the Sundays after Trinity, and the punctuation marks of saints' days.

We go on to examine the principal features of the Eucharist, in more detail than in the comments alongside the words of the service: the collect or opening prayer and its companion, the post communion prayer; the Gloria and the Nicene Creed; the reading of the Bible; the Lord's Prayer. We explore the shape and history of the eucharistic prayer at the heart of the service. And we look at what it means to remember Jesus's words and actions at the Last Supper and what this means to us as we receive his body and blood in the sacrament. Finally, we explore the Dismissal, and the connections between the sacrament and the rest of our lives.

The Eucharist is rich in meaning: there are many aspects to it and many ways of looking at it. In the Eucharist the local Christian community comes together as the body of Christ. Together the people celebrate, hearing readings from the Bible and then taking bread and wine, blessing them and receiving Christ's body and blood. The model for this service is the Last Supper at which, on the night before he died, Jesus did this with his disciples. The Eucharist is also foreshadowed in the teaching of Jesus, in many of his parables, and in many of his miracles. Here we receive Christ the bread of life, and Christ the true vine. And in receiving, we catch a glimpse of the kingdom of God, of the angels singing 'Holy, holy, holy' before his throne, and of the great feast, the wedding banquet of the Lamb of God, to which all the faithful are invited. Come to the Feast!

GILL AMBROSE
SIMON KERSHAW
Cambridge, August 2001

Page Numbers

Come to the Feast contains the full text of Holy Communion Order One from *Common Worship*. The pages from *Common Worship* have two sets of page numbers. The outer numbers are the page numbers of *Come to the Feast*, while the inner numbers near the centre of most of these pages refer to the equivalent pages in *Common Worship: Services and Prayers for the Church of England*.

Part One

The Order for the Celebration of
Holy Communion
also called
The Eucharist
and
The Lord's Supper

In the first part of the service we are brought together as the assembly by joining in prayer and praise, and by remembering our sins, and we prepare to listen to the Word of God.

God calls us to worship him and we gather in his name. The baptized community comes together for the service: in Matthew 28:19, Jesus tells his disciples to baptize all nations in the name of the Father, Son and Holy Spirit.

This greeting has ancient roots in both the early Christian tradition (2 Thessalonians 3:16) and the Jewish tradition (Ruth 2:4).

A New Testament greeting: see, for example, 1 Timothy 1:2; 2 Timothy 1:2; 2 John 3.

Eastertide is the crown of the Church's year and it is appropriately marked with its own acclamation of the risen Christ.

Only after greeting in the Lord's name are more informal words of welcome said.

Order One

¶ *The Gathering*

At the entry of the ministers a hymn may be sung.

The president may say

In the name of the Father,
and of the Son,
and of the Holy Spirit.

All **Amen.**

The Greeting

The president greets the people

The Lord be with you
All **and also with you.**

(or)

Grace, mercy and peace
from God our Father
and the Lord Jesus Christ
be with you
All **and also with you.**

From Easter Day to Pentecost this acclamation follows

Alleluia. Christ is risen.
All **He is risen indeed. Alleluia.**

Words of welcome or introduction may be said.

This prayer, traditionally called the Collect for Purity, is a prayer for 'purity of intention' as we prepare to meet God in the Eucharist. It can be used as a preparation before the service if not used here.

See the Form of Preparation, pages 107–115, and the Examination of Conscience, pages 112, 114.

Mark 12:29–31: this summary is the heart of Jesus's teaching, and gives us a perspective on where we fall short. Matthew 22:37–40 and Luke 10:25–28 also describe this in a slightly different form.

John 3:16 and 1 John 2:1 remind us that Jesus not only died for us, but also continues to plead for us with the Father.

If there is a silence, then we call to mind our shortcomings.

Prayer of Preparation

This prayer may be said

All   **Almighty God,**
to whom all hearts are open,
all desires known,
and from whom no secrets are hidden:
cleanse the thoughts of our hearts
by the inspiration of your Holy Spirit,
that we may perfectly love you,
and worthily magnify your holy name;
through Christ our Lord.
Amen.

Prayers of Penitence

The Commandments, the Comfortable Words, the Beatitudes
(pages 93–99 and 109–113) or the following Summary of the Law
may be used

Our Lord Jesus Christ said:
The first commandment is this:
'Hear, O Israel, the Lord our God is the only Lord.
You shall love the Lord your God with all your heart,
with all your soul, with all your mind,
and with all your strength.'

The second is this: 'Love your neighbour as yourself.'
There is no other commandment greater than these.
On these two commandments hang all the law and the prophets.

All   **Amen. Lord, have mercy.**

A minister uses a seasonal invitation to confession or these or other
suitable words

God so loved the world
that he gave his only Son Jesus Christ
to save us from our sins,
to be our advocate in heaven,
and to bring us to eternal life.

Let us confess our sins in penitence and faith,
firmly resolved to keep God's commandments
and to live in love and peace with all.

We remember the sins we have each committed as an individual, and the sins we have committed collectively. See Chapter 4 *Eucharistic Community, Personal Devotion*, page 128. We turn from the past and promise to make a new start.

Confession goes hand in hand with a determination to try to do better.

A reminder of the Summary of the Law (pages 17, 111) which bids us to 'Love the Lord your God with your whole heart' and 'Love your neighbour as yourself.'

In Micah 6:8, the prophet tells us what God requires of those who follow him.

All **Almighty God, our heavenly Father,**
we have sinned against you
and against our neighbour
in thought and word and deed,
through negligence, through weakness,
through our own deliberate fault.
We are truly sorry
and repent of all our sins.
For the sake of your Son Jesus Christ,
who died for us,
forgive us all that is past
and grant that we may serve you in newness of life
to the glory of your name.
Amen.

(or)

All **Most merciful God,**
Father of our Lord Jesus Christ,
we confess that we have sinned
in thought, word and deed.
We have not loved you with our whole heart.
We have not loved our neighbours as ourselves.
In your mercy
forgive what we have been,
help us to amend what we are,
and direct what we shall be;
that we may do justly,
love mercy,
and walk humbly with you, our God.
Amen.

The Greek words *kyrie eleison*, meaning 'Lord have mercy,' are a plea for God to have pity on us and to hear our prayer.

The president, speaking with the authority of the Church, prays that God will forgive us. Matthew 16:13–19 assures us that Christ has given this authority to his Church and that God does forgive us.

The president's words make it clear that God's forgiveness is conditional on our repentance – our intention to turn from our sins.

Or, with suitable penitential sentences, the Kyrie eleison may be used

Lord, have mercy.

All **Lord, have mercy.**

Christ, have mercy.

All **Christ, have mercy.**

Lord, have mercy.

All **Lord, have mercy.**

If another confession has already been used, the Kyrie eleison may be used without interpolation here or after the absolution.

The president says

Almighty God,
who forgives all who truly repent,
have mercy upon *you*,
pardon and deliver *you* from all *your* sins,
confirm and strengthen *you* in all goodness,
and keep *you* in life eternal;
through Jesus Christ our Lord.

All **Amen.**

In this ancient Christian hymn we join with the angels and with Christians past, present and future, in praising God and celebrating Christ as our Saviour. For more on the Gloria see Chapter 6 *Glory to God: the Gloria in Excelsis*, page 134.

The song of the angels praising God at the birth of Jesus (Luke 2:14) is followed by an acclamation praising God the Father, and two acclamations praising God the Son.

In John 1:29,36, John the Baptist acclaims Jesus as the Lamb of God who takes away the sin of the world – a title which looks back to the Passover sacrifice of a lamb, and forward to the triumphant Lamb of the Book of Revelation. It reminds us that in the Eucharist we are united with the tradition we inherit, and the hope our faith holds before us.

We acclaim Jesus as 'Lord', acknowledging that he is fully God.

The *Gathering* culminates in the *Collect*, a prayer which gathers together, or 'collects', the opening devotions. A collect is provided for each Sunday and for other holy days. See Chapter 7 *Praying Together: the Collect*, page 135.

In the silence we can pray for any special intentions, individual or communal, before the president gathers the prayers together.

Gloria in Excelsis

The Gloria in excelsis may be used

All **Glory to God in the highest,
and peace to his people on earth.**

**Lord God, heavenly King,
almighty God and Father,
we worship you, we give you thanks,
we praise you for your glory.**

**Lord Jesus Christ, only Son of the Father,
Lord God, Lamb of God,
you take away the sin of the world:
have mercy on us;
you are seated at the right hand of the Father:
receive our prayer.**

**For you alone are the Holy One,
you alone are the Lord,
you alone are the Most High, Jesus Christ,
with the Holy Spirit,
in the glory of God the Father.
Amen.**

The Collect

*The president introduces a period of silent prayer with the words
'Let us pray' or a more specific bidding.*

The Collect is said, and all respond

All **Amen.**

In the second part of the service, we listen together to the Word of God in the Bible readings and sermon, and pray together in the intercessions.

The choice of readings is generally from the lectionary so that we hear a wide range of Scripture. See Chapter 8 *Listening to the Word: the Lectionary*, page 136.

In the Old Testament we hear the Bible as Jesus and his contemporaries knew it, the story of how the Jews came to understand God's covenant with them.

The psalm, often said or sung with a congregational response, reflects on the Old Testament reading. The New Testament reading is usually from one of the letters, or 'epistles', of the apostles to the young Church.

The gospel reading proclaims the good news of Jesus as recorded by the evangelists. The proclamation of the good news is central to this part of the service (the *Liturgy of the Word*) and special attention is often drawn to it: we stand and turn to face the reader; the gospel may be proclaimed from the middle of the congregation, and there may be a procession with candles; 'Alleluia' (or in Lent another acclamation) may be sung and the responses are different from those for the other readings; the gospel book might have been carried into the church at the start of the service, and may be censed. All these draw attention, not to the book or the reader, but to the proclamation of the gospel, and acknowledge Christ, the Word of God, as present in the reading of his gospel.

After the readings there may be a period of silent reflection.

The sermon generally provides an opportunity to explore the readings further. For example, it may explain or teach or nurture or give pastoral guidance or encourage devotion.

¶ *The Liturgy of the Word*

Readings

Either one or two readings from Scripture precede the Gospel reading.

At the end of each the reader may say

This is the word of the Lord.

All **Thanks be to God.**

The psalm or canticle follows the first reading; other hymns and songs may be used between the readings.

Gospel Reading

An acclamation may herald the Gospel reading.

When the Gospel is announced the reader says

Hear the Gospel of our Lord Jesus Christ according to N.

All **Glory to you, O Lord.**

At the end

This is the Gospel of the Lord.

All **Praise to you, O Christ.**

Sermon

In the creed we join with Christians across the world and throughout history in stating the beliefs of the Church. We acknowledge God as Trinity: Father, Son and Holy Spirit, responding to the reading of the gospel, and the teaching of the sermon.

The creed expresses what the Church came to understand about Christ, and how the man who was born of Mary and crucified under Pilate is at the same time the Son of God through whom all things were made, yet who died for our sake. It affirms that God is also present as God the Holy Spirit. It reminds us of the importance of the Church and our baptism, and of the hope of the resurrection.

See Chapter 9 *We Believe: the Nicene Creed*, page 139 for more information on the creed.

The Creed

*On Sundays and Principal Holy Days an authorized translation of
the Nicene Creed is used, or on occasion the Apostles' Creed (page 101)
or an authorized Affirmation of Faith may be used (see pages 138–148
in* Common Worship: Services and Prayers for the Church of England*).*

All **We believe in one God,
the Father, the Almighty,
maker of heaven and earth,
of all that is,
seen and unseen.**

**We believe in one Lord, Jesus Christ,
the only Son of God,
eternally begotten of the Father,
God from God, Light from Light,
true God from true God,
begotten, not made,
of one Being with the Father;
through him all things were made.
For us and for our salvation he came down from heaven,
was incarnate from the Holy Spirit and the Virgin Mary
and was made man.
For our sake he was crucified under Pontius Pilate;
he suffered death and was buried.
On the third day he rose again
in accordance with the Scriptures;
he ascended into heaven
and is seated at the right hand of the Father.
He will come again in glory to judge the living and the dead,
and his kingdom will have no end.**

**We believe in the Holy Spirit,
the Lord, the giver of life,
who proceeds from the Father and the Son,
who with the Father and the Son is worshipped and glorified,
who has spoken through the prophets.
We believe in one holy catholic and apostolic Church.
We acknowledge one baptism for the forgiveness of sins.
We look for the resurrection of the dead,
and the life of the world to come.
Amen.**

We have heard the readings, listened to the sermon, and proclaimed the creed. Our response is to turn to God in prayer. We bring our concerns to him, whether global, local or personal, and leave them in his hands.

The intercessions may be led by the president or another minister, or it may be appropriate for them to be led by one or more members of the congregation.

These responses express our confidence in our Lord Jesus Christ as our advocate and mediator (see 1 John 2:1,2).

Just as the first section of the service, the *Gathering*, ends in prayer with a collect, so this second part, the *Liturgy of the Word*, may also end in a collect, or else this short petition, which gathers together the prayers of the people.

Prayers of Intercession

One of the forms on pages 281–289 in Common Worship: Services and Prayers for the Church of England *or other suitable words may be used.*

The prayers usually include these concerns and may follow this sequence:

¶ *The Church of Christ*

¶ *Creation, human society, the Sovereign and those in authority*

¶ *The local community*

¶ *Those who suffer*

¶ *The communion of saints*

These responses may be used

Lord, in your mercy
All **hear our prayer.**

(or)

Lord, hear us.
All **Lord, graciously hear us.**

And at the end

Merciful Father,
All **accept these prayers
for the sake of your Son,
our Saviour Jesus Christ.
Amen.**

The third part of the service now begins, in which the bread and wine are taken and blessed, broken and shared in the sacrament of communion.

The section usually begins with the exchange of the Peace, though this may also take place elsewhere in the service. It is Christ's peace, shared with his disciples (see, for example, John 20:19,20) and which we now share with one another. The biblical introductions indicate how important this is.

The *Preparation of the Table* is a necessary practical step. The bread and wine, and other gifts, may be presented by representatives of the congregation – they are the work of human hands and we all share in providing them.

Prayers may be said here (see page 103), but we should remember that it is in the eucharistic prayer itself that we give thanks for the bread and wine.

When the table is prepared, the president takes the bread and wine from the table and replaces them, indicating that these are the items which will be removed from their ordinary everyday use and transformed in the eucharistic prayer.

¶ *The Liturgy of the Sacrament*

The Peace

*The president may introduce the Peace with a suitable sentence,
and then says*

The peace of the Lord be always with you

All **and also with you.**

These words may be added
Let us offer one another a sign of peace.

All may exchange a sign of peace.

Preparation of the Table
Taking of the Bread and Wine

A hymn may be sung.

The gifts of the people may be gathered and presented.

The table is prepared and bread and wine are placed upon it.

One or more of the prayers at the preparation of the table may be said.

The president takes the bread and wine.

The eucharistic prayer is at the heart of the service. In it we give thanks for God's goodness, we remember all that he has done for our salvation, especially in Jesus Christ, and we pray for the gift of the Holy Spirit.

See Chapter 10 *Thanks and Praise: the Eucharistic Prayer*, page 141, for more information.

This is a prayer of rejoicing: our hearts are lifted up in praise to God, remembering some of the things that the Father has done in creating and redeeming the world.

In response we join with the song of the angels, recorded in Isaiah's great vision (Isaiah 6:3), and sung in the Temple in Jerusalem. The hymn may be followed by the acclamation of the people of Jerusalem at the entry of Christ to the city on the first Palm Sunday (Matthew 21:9; Mark 11:9–10; Luke 19:38; John 12:13).

We focus on the actions of Jesus, and in remembering the Last Supper, we are mystically present with Christ and he with us in one great celebration, undivided by time and space.

At the heart of the prayer, we acclaim Christ's death and resurrection, the victory of the cross remembered in broken bread and wine outpoured.

The acclamation 'When we eat this bread...' is from 1 Corinthians 11:26.

As the prayer continues we pray that God the Holy Spirit will be on us and the gifts of bread and wine.

The prayer ends as it began – in praise of God – and we make the prayer our own, adding our joyful 'Amen'.

The Eucharistic Prayer

An authorized Eucharistic Prayer is used (pages 49–91).

The president says

The Lord be with you	*(or)*	The Lord is here.
All **and also with you.**		**His Spirit is with us.**

Lift up your hearts.
All   **We lift them to the Lord.**

Let us give thanks to the Lord our God.
All   **It is right to give thanks and praise.**

The president praises God for his mighty acts and all respond

All   **Holy, holy, holy Lord,**
        God of power and might,
        heaven and earth are full of your glory.
        Hosanna in the highest.
        [Blessed is he who comes in the name of the Lord.
        Hosanna in the highest.]

The president recalls the Last Supper,
and one of these four acclamations may be used

[Great is the mystery of faith:]	[Praise to you, Lord Jesus:]
All **Christ has died:**	**Dying you destroyed**
Christ is risen:	**our death,**
Christ will come again.	**rising you restored our life:**
	Lord Jesus, come in glory.

[Christ is the bread of life:]	[Jesus Christ is Lord:]
All **When we eat this bread**	**Lord, by your cross and**
and drink this cup,	**resurrection**
we proclaim your death,	**you have set us free.**
Lord Jesus,	**You are the Saviour of the**
until you come in glory.	**world.**

The Prayer continues and leads into the doxology,
to which all respond boldly

All   **Amen.**

In the various prayers there are different congregational responses.

Prayers A, D and G end with words from the Song to the Lamb from Revelation 5:13.

In Prayer F the responses catch the fervour and excitement of the Eastern Orthodox prayer of St Basil.

Prayer H is a dialogue between the president and the congregation. It climaxes in the 'Holy, holy, holy' of the Sanctus. See the note on page 32.

Prayer A
page 49

This response may be used

All **To you be glory and praise for ever.**

and the Prayer ends

All **Blessing and honour and glory and power
be yours for ever and ever.
Amen.**

Prayer D
page 69

These words are used

This is his/our story.

All **This is our song:
Hosanna in the highest.**

and the Prayer ends

All **Blessing and honour and glory and power
be yours for ever and ever.
Amen.**

Prayer F
page 77

These responses may be used

All **Amen. Lord, we believe.**

All **Amen. Come, Lord Jesus.**

All **Amen. Come, Holy Spirit.**

Prayer G
page 83

Prayer G ends

All **Blessing and honour and glory and power
be yours for ever and ever.
Amen.**

Prayer H
page 89

For Prayer H, see page 89.

In the Lord's Prayer, taught by Christ to his disciples (Matthew 6:9–13; Luke 11:2–4), we pray for the coming of God's kingdom and for the bread that God gives us – especially appropriate at the Eucharist where we receive the bread of life as a foretaste of the banquet in the kingdom of God.

See Chapter 12 *Our Father: the Lord's Prayer*, page 148.

The Lord's Prayer

As our Saviour taught us, so we pray

All **Our Father in heaven,**
hallowed be your name,
your kingdom come,
your will be done,
on earth as in heaven.
Give us today our daily bread.
Forgive us our sins
as we forgive those who sin against us.
Lead us not into temptation
but deliver us from evil.
For the kingdom, the power,
and the glory are yours
now and for ever.
Amen.

(or)

Let us pray with confidence as our Saviour has taught us

All **Our Father, who art in heaven,**
hallowed be thy name;
thy kingdom come;
thy will be done;
on earth as it is in heaven.
Give us this day our daily bread.
And forgive us our trespasses,
as we forgive those who trespass against us.
And lead us not into temptation;
but deliver us from evil.
For thine is the kingdom,
the power and the glory,
for ever and ever.
Amen.

We have taken and blessed the bread and wine. Now the bread is broken so that it can be shared and as a symbol of Christ's body, broken on the cross. The words from 1 Corinthians 10:17 remind us that together we are the body of Christ, and we mystically share the bread, the body of Christ.

The alternative words from 1 Corinthians 11:26 again link the Eucharist with the remembrance of Christ's death and the promise of the coming kingdom.

The anthem 'Lamb of God' is a further reminder of the Passover sacrifice of a lamb (Exodus 12). See Chapter 11 *Remembrance and Sacrifice: the Eucharistic Prayer*, page 145. In the New Testament, John the Baptist acclaimed Jesus as the Lamb of God (John 1:29, 35).

Breaking of the Bread

The president breaks the consecrated bread.

We break this bread
to share in the body of Christ.

All **Though we are many, we are one body,
because we all share in one bread.**

(or)

Every time we eat this bread
and drink this cup,

All **we proclaim the Lord's death
until he comes.**

The Agnus Dei may be used as the bread is broken

All **Lamb of God,
you take away the sin of the world,
have mercy on us.**

**Lamb of God,
you take away the sin of the world,
have mercy on us.**

**Lamb of God,
you take away the sin of the world,
grant us peace.**

(or)

All **Jesus, Lamb of God,
have mercy on us.**

**Jesus, bearer of our sins,
have mercy on us.**

**Jesus, redeemer of the world,
grant us peace.**

We have taken and blessed the bread and wine, and the bread has been broken. Now we share the consecrated bread and wine, receiving the body and blood of Christ, remembering that they were given and shed for us.

These words emphasise those just used in the *Agnus Dei* (John 1:29, 35) and remind us again of the wedding feast in God's kingdom (Revelation 19:9). The response is adapted from that given by the centurion who asked Jesus to heal his servant (Matthew 8:8).

An invitation in the form of an acclamation from the liturgy of the Orthodox Church.

The special form for Easter is from 1 Corinthians 5:7–8.

Giving of Communion

The president says one of these invitations to communion

Draw near with faith.
Receive the body of our Lord Jesus Christ
which he gave for you,
and his blood which he shed for you.
Eat and drink
in remembrance that he died for you,
and feed on him in your hearts
by faith with thanksgiving.

(or)

Jesus is the Lamb of God
who takes away the sin of the world.
Blessed are those who are called to his supper.

All   **Lord, I am not worthy to receive you,
but only say the word, and I shall be healed.**

(or)

God's holy gifts
for God's holy people.

All   **Jesus Christ is holy,
Jesus Christ is Lord,
to the glory of God the Father.**

or, from Easter Day to Pentecost

Alleluia. Christ our passover is sacrificed for us.

All   **Therefore let us keep the feast. Alleluia.**

Like the response to the second invitation above, this optional prayer starts from our unworthiness to receive God's holy gifts. Only by God's grace are we able to do so (Matthew 15:27; Mark 7:28). But we are cleansed by the body and blood of Christ (John 6:56) to abide with him for ever.

The alternative version of the same prayer is worthy of further study and meditation. There are hints of the parable of the wedding feast told in Matthew 22:1–10 and Luke 14:16–24; of Psalm 24:3–4 and James 4:8; of the woman in Matthew 15:27 and Mark 7:28; and of the meal with sinners in Matthew 9:11.

As we wait to receive the sacrament we may use one of these prayers, or another, such as these words of George Herbert:

> Love bade me welcome; yet my soul drew back,
> > Guilty of dust and sin.
> But quick-eyed Love, observing me grow slack
> > From my first entrance in,
> Drew nearer to me, sweetly questioning
> > If I lacked anything.
>
> 'A guest,' I answered, 'worthy to be here.'
> > Love said, 'You shall be he.'
> 'I, the unkind, ungrateful? Ah, my dear,
> > I cannot look on thee.'
> Love took my hand, and smiling did reply,
> > 'Who made the eyes but I?'
>
> 'Truth, Lord, but I have marred them; let my shame
> > Go where it doth deserve.'
> 'And know you not,' says Love, 'who bore the blame?'
> > 'My dear, then I will serve.'
> 'You must sit down,' says Love, 'and taste my meat.'
> > So I did sit and eat.
> > > George Herbert (1593–1633)

Some other prayers are provided on page 116.

As we receive the sacrament we say 'Amen', responding in faith to God's gift of his Son for our salvation.

One of these prayers may be said before the distribution

All **We do not presume**
to come to this your table, merciful Lord,
trusting in our own righteousness,
but in your manifold and great mercies.
We are not worthy
so much as to gather up the crumbs under your table.
But you are the same Lord
whose nature is always to have mercy.
Grant us therefore, gracious Lord,
so to eat the flesh of your dear Son Jesus Christ
and to drink his blood,
that our sinful bodies may be made clean by his body
and our souls washed through his most precious blood,
and that we may evermore dwell in him, and he in us.
Amen.

(or)

All **Most merciful Lord,**
your love compels us to come in.
Our hands were unclean,
our hearts were unprepared;
we were not fit
even to eat the crumbs from under your table.
But you, Lord, are the God of our salvation,
and share your bread with sinners.
So cleanse and feed us
with the precious body and blood of your Son,
that he may live in us and we in him;
and that we, with the whole company of Christ,
may sit and eat in your kingdom.
Amen.

The president and people receive communion.

Authorized words of distribution are used and the communicant replies

Amen.

During the distribution hymns and anthems may be sung.

Now we have taken and blessed the bread and wine. We have broken the bread, and shared the bread and wine. We have been fed with the most holy food, nourished with the body and blood of our Lord Jesus Christ. And so we pray and give thanks. The words of many communion hymns and other prayers are appropriate (see pages 105 and 116–118).

There may be a period of silence after communion in which to reflect and pray.

The Gathering ended with a collect, and the Liturgy of the Word also ended in a collect. So too does the Liturgy of the Sacrament with a post communion prayer said by the president (see Chapter 7 Praying Together: the Collect, page 135), and sometimes a congregational prayer.

The first of these congregational prayers links thanksgiving with a reminder that we are a sacrifice (Romans 12:1), and that helped by the Holy Spirit we are the body of Christ in the world.

The second prayer contains many references, worth further meditation. It alludes to the story of the prodigal son in Luke 15:11–32 (especially verse 20). The Spirit lights us – it both enlightens and inflames us. We should not keep this light under a bushel (Matthew 5:14–16), but use it to enlighten the world.

These prayers, and those on pages 105 and 116–118, can also be used for private devotion after communion.

*If either or both of the consecrated elements are likely to prove
insufficient, the president returns to the holy table and adds more,
saying the words on page 296 in* Common Worship: Services and
Prayers for the Church of England.

*Any consecrated bread and wine which is not required for purposes
of communion is consumed at the end of the distribution or after
the service.*

Prayer after Communion

Silence is kept.

The Post Communion or another suitable prayer is said.

All may say one of these prayers

All **Almighty God,
we thank you for feeding us
with the body and blood of your Son Jesus Christ.
Through him we offer you our souls and bodies
to be a living sacrifice.
Send us out
in the power of your Spirit
to live and work
to your praise and glory.
Amen.**

(or)

All **Father of all,
we give you thanks and praise,
that when we were still far off
you met us in your Son and brought us home.
Dying and living, he declared your love,
gave us grace, and opened the gate of glory.
May we who share Christ's body live his risen life;
we who drink his cup bring life to others;
we whom the Spirit lights give light to the world.
Keep us firm in the hope you have set before us,
so we and all your children shall be free,
and the whole earth live to praise your name;
through Christ our Lord.
Amen.**

After communion the service ends quickly. There may be announcements and notices, reminding us of things to take out into the world, or to nurture our faith in the days ahead.

This blessing is introduced with words from Philippians 4:7, the president praying that God's blessing will be with us always.

The service had a clear beginning, now it has a clear end. We are to go out, empowered by the body and blood of Christ, in communion with one another. We can love and serve the Lord only in the name of Christ.

See Chapter 13 *Go in Peace: the Dismissal*, page 151.

At Eastertide we leave the service with 'Alleluia' ringing in our ears.

¶ The Dismissal

A hymn may be sung.

The president may use the seasonal blessing, or another suitable blessing

(or)

The peace of God,
which passes all understanding,
keep your hearts and minds
in the knowledge and love of God,
and of his Son Jesus Christ our Lord;
and the blessing of God almighty,
the Father, the Son, and the Holy Spirit,
be among you and remain with you always.

All   **Amen.**

A minister says

Go in peace to love and serve the Lord.

All   **In the name of Christ. Amen.**

(or)

Go in the peace of Christ.

All   **Thanks be to God.**

or, from Easter Day to Pentecost

Go in the peace of Christ. Alleluia, alleluia.

All   **Thanks be to God. Alleluia, alleluia.**

The ministers and people depart.

See Chapter 10 *Thanks and Praise: the Eucharistic Prayer*, page 141, for more information on the eucharistic prayers. Here, attention is drawn to the components of each prayer.

Prayer A is loosely based on the prayer in the third-century *Apostolic Tradition*. It was largely written in 1972 for the revision which led to the *Alternative Service Book* 1980.

The Preface: we praise God for his goodness.

We remember God's mighty acts. This preface reminds us of our redemption in words similar to those of the creed. There may be a seasonal preface instead of these words.

¶ Eucharistic Prayers for use in Order One

Proper Prefaces are to be found on pages 294 and 300–329 in
Common Worship: Services and Prayers for the Church of England.

Prayer A

*If an extended Preface is used, it replaces all words between the opening
dialogue and the Sanctus.*

	The Lord be with you	*(or)*	The Lord is here.
All	**and also with you.**		**His Spirit is with us.**

Lift up your hearts.
All **We lift them to the Lord.**

Let us give thanks to the Lord our God.
All **It is right to give thanks and praise.**

It is indeed right,
it is our duty and our joy,
at all times and in all places
to give you thanks and praise,
holy Father, heavenly King,
almighty and eternal God,
through Jesus Christ your Son our Lord.

The following may be omitted if a short Proper Preface is used

For he is your living Word;
through him you have created all things from the beginning,
and formed us in your own image.

[*All* **To you be glory and praise for ever.**]

Through him you have freed us from the slavery of sin,
giving him to be born of a woman and to die upon the cross;
you raised him from the dead
and exalted him to your right hand on high.

[*All* **To you be glory and praise for ever.**]

Through him you have sent upon us
your holy and life-giving Spirit,
and made us a people for your own possession.

[*All* **To you be glory and praise for ever.**]

The *Sanctus*: we join with the song of the angels, recorded in Isaiah's great vision (Isaiah 6:3), and sung in the Temple in Jerusalem. The hymn may be followed by the acclamation of the people of Jerusalem at the entry of Christ to the city on the first Palm Sunday (Matthew 21:9; Mark 11:9–10; Luke 19:38; John 12:13).

The *epiclesis*: we invoke the power of God the Holy Spirit. The prayer moves from *praise* to *petition*.

The *institution narrative*: we recall the Last Supper and Jesus's identification of the bread and wine as his body and blood.

Short Proper Preface, when appropriate

Therefore with angels and archangels,
and with all the company of heaven,
we proclaim your great and glorious name,
for ever praising you and *saying:*

All **Holy, holy, holy Lord,**
God of power and might,
heaven and earth are full of your glory.
Hosanna in the highest.
[Blessed is he who comes in the name of the Lord.
Hosanna in the highest.]

Accept our praises, heavenly Father,
through your Son our Saviour Jesus Christ,
and as we follow his example and obey his command,
grant that by the power of your Holy Spirit
these gifts of bread and wine
may be to us his body and his blood;

who, in the same night that he was betrayed,
took bread and gave you thanks;
he broke it and gave it to his disciples, saying:
Take, eat; this is my body which is given for you;
do this in remembrance of me.

[*All* **To you be glory and praise for ever.]**

In the same way, after supper
he took the cup and gave you thanks;
he gave it to them, saying:
Drink this, all of you;
this is my blood of the new covenant,
which is shed for you and for many for the forgiveness of sins.
Do this, as often as you drink it,
in remembrance of me.

[*All* **To you be glory and praise for ever.]**

The anamnesis: we identify our action now as the fulfilment of Christ's command, linking the Last Supper with the crucifixion and with us as we pray.

This acclamation is from 1 Corinthians 11:26.

Therefore, heavenly Father,
we remember his offering of himself
made once for all upon the cross;
we proclaim his mighty resurrection and glorious ascension;
we look for the coming of your kingdom,
and with this bread and this cup
we make the memorial of Christ your Son our Lord.

One of these four acclamations is used

[Great is the mystery of faith:]

All   **Christ has died:**
     Christ is risen:
     Christ will come again.

(or)

[Praise to you, Lord Jesus:]

All   **Dying you destroyed our death,**
     rising you restored our life:
     Lord Jesus, come in glory.

(or)

[Christ is the bread of life:]

All   **When we eat this bread and drink this cup,**
     we proclaim your death, Lord Jesus,
     until you come in glory.

(or)

[Jesus Christ is Lord:]

All   **Lord, by your cross and resurrection**
     you have set us free.
     You are the Saviour of the world.

Again we invoke the Holy Spirit, praying that we shall receive the benefits of the sacramental meal.

The prayer ends in praise with the doxology...

... culminating in the song from Revelation 5:1 3.

Accept through him, our great high priest,
this our sacrifice of thanks and praise,
and as we eat and drink these holy gifts
in the presence of your divine majesty,
renew us by your Spirit,
inspire us with your love
and unite us in the body of your Son,
Jesus Christ our Lord.

[*All*   **To you be glory and praise for ever.**]

Through him, and with him, and in him,
in the unity of the Holy Spirit,
with all who stand before you in earth and heaven,
we worship you, Father almighty,
in songs of everlasting praise:

All   **Blessing and honour and glory and power
be yours for ever and ever.
Amen.**

The service continues with the Lord's Prayer on page 37.

Prayer B is derived from the third-century *Apostolic Tradition*. It is closer to the original than the version in Prayer A.

The Preface: we praise God for his goodness.

We remember God's mighty acts. This preface reminds us of our redemption in the life, death and resurrection of Jesus Christ. It may be replaced by a seasonal preface.

The Sanctus: we join with the song of the angels, recorded in Isaiah's great vision (Isaiah 6:3), and sung in the Temple in Jerusalem. The hymn may be followed by the acclamation of the people of Jerusalem at the entry of Christ to the city on the first Palm Sunday (Matthew 21:9; Mark 11:9–10; Luke 19:38; John 12:13).

Prayer B

If an extended Preface is used, it replaces all words between the opening dialogue and the Sanctus.

The Lord be with you   *(or)*   The Lord is here.

All **and also with you.**   **His Spirit is with us.**

Lift up your hearts.

All **We lift them to the Lord.**

Let us give thanks to the Lord our God.

All **It is right to give thanks and praise.**

Father, we give you thanks and praise
through your beloved Son Jesus Christ, your living Word,
through whom you have created all things;
who was sent by you in your great goodness to be our Saviour.

By the power of the Holy Spirit he took flesh;
as your Son, born of the blessed Virgin,
he lived on earth and went about among us;
he opened wide his arms for us on the cross;
he put an end to death by dying for us;
and revealed the resurrection by rising to new life;
so he fulfilled your will and won for you a holy people.

Short Proper Preface, when appropriate

Therefore with angels and archangels,
and with all the company of heaven,
we proclaim your great and glorious name,
for ever praising you and *saying:*

All **Holy, holy, holy Lord,**
God of power and might,
heaven and earth are full of your glory.
Hosanna in the highest.
[Blessed is he who comes in the name of the Lord.
Hosanna in the highest.]

The epiclesis: we invoke the power of God the Holy Spirit. The prayer moves from *praise* to *petition.*

The institution narrative: we recall the Last Supper and Jesus's identification of the bread and wine as his body and blood.

This acclamation is from 1 Corinthians 11:26.

Lord, you are holy indeed, the source of all holiness;
grant that by the power of your Holy Spirit,
and according to your holy will,
these gifts of bread and wine
may be to us the body and blood of our Lord Jesus Christ;

who, in the same night that he was betrayed,
took bread and gave you thanks;
he broke it and gave it to his disciples, saying:
Take, eat; this is my body which is given for you;
do this in remembrance of me.

In the same way, after supper
he took the cup and gave you thanks;
he gave it to them, saying:
Drink this, all of you;
this is my blood of the new covenant,
which is shed for you and for many for the forgiveness of sins.
Do this, as often as you drink it,
in remembrance of me.

One of these four acclamations is used

[Great is the mystery of faith:]

All **Christ has died:**
Christ is risen:
Christ will come again.

(or)

[Praise to you, Lord Jesus:]

All **Dying you destroyed our death,**
rising you restored our life:
Lord Jesus, come in glory.

(or)

[Christ is the bread of life:]

All **When we eat this bread and drink this cup,**
we proclaim your death, Lord Jesus,
until you come in glory.

(or)

[Jesus Christ is Lord:]

All **Lord, by your cross and resurrection**
you have set us free.
You are the Saviour of the world.

The anamnesis: we identify our action now as the fulfilment of Christ's command, linking the Last Supper with the crucifixion and with us as we pray.

Again we invoke the Holy Spirit, praying that we shall receive the benefits of the sacramental meal.

The prayer ends in praise with *the doxology*...

... to which we all respond 'Amen'.

And so, Father, calling to mind his death on the cross,
his perfect sacrifice made once for the sins of the whole world;
rejoicing in his mighty resurrection and glorious ascension,
and looking for his coming in glory,
we celebrate this memorial of our redemption.
As we offer you this our sacrifice of praise and thanksgiving,
we bring before you this bread and this cup
and we thank you for counting us worthy
to stand in your presence and serve you.

Send the Holy Spirit on your people
and gather into one in your kingdom
all who share this one bread and one cup,
so that we, in the company of [N and] all the saints,
may praise and glorify you for ever,
through Jesus Christ our Lord;

by whom, and with whom, and in whom,
in the unity of the Holy Spirit,
all honour and glory be yours, almighty Father,
for ever and ever.

All   **Amen.**

The service continues with the Lord's Prayer on page 37.

Prayer C is derived from the prayer in the 1662 *Book of Common Prayer*, written by Archbishop Cranmer for the 1552 prayer book.

The Preface: we briefly praise God for his goodness.

This preface concentrates on the atoning death of Christ on the cross and reminds us of our redemption. It may be replaced by a seasonal preface.

The Sanctus: we join with the song of the angels, recorded in Isaiah's great vision (Isaiah 6:3), and sung in the Temple in Jerusalem. The hymn may be followed by the acclamation of the people of Jerusalem at the entry of Christ to the city on the first Palm Sunday (Matthew 21:9; Mark 11:9–10; Luke 19:38; John 12:13).

Prayer C

The Lord be with you   *(or)*   The Lord is here.
All **and also with you.**   **His Spirit is with us.**

Lift up your hearts.
All **We lift them to the Lord.**

Let us give thanks to the Lord our God.
All **It is right to give thanks and praise.**

It is indeed right,
it is our duty and our joy,
at all times and in all places
to give you thanks and praise,
holy Father, heavenly King,
almighty and eternal God,
through Jesus Christ our Lord.

Short Proper Preface, when appropriate

[or, when there is no Proper Preface

For he is our great high priest,
who has loosed us from our sins
and has made us to be a royal priesthood to you,
our God and Father.]

Therefore with angels and archangels,
and with all the company of heaven,
we proclaim your great and glorious name,
for ever praising you and *saying:*

All **Holy, holy, holy Lord,**
God of power and might,
heaven and earth are full of your glory.
Hosanna in the highest.
[Blessed is he who comes in the name of the Lord.
Hosanna in the highest.]

Christ's death and its role in our salvation are linked to the Last Supper and to this celebration.

The *epiclesis*: we invoke the power of God the Holy Spirit, emphasising that it is in sharing the sacrament that we share in the benefits. The prayer moves from *praise* to *petition*.

The *institution narrative*: we recall the Last Supper and Jesus's identification of the bread and wine as his body and blood.

The acclamation 'When we eat this bread...' is from I Corinthians 11:26.

All glory be to you, our heavenly Father,
who, in your tender mercy,
gave your only Son our Saviour Jesus Christ
to suffer death upon the cross for our redemption;
who made there by his one oblation of himself once offered
a full, perfect and sufficient sacrifice, oblation and satisfaction
for the sins of the whole world;
he instituted, and in his holy gospel commanded us to continue,
a perpetual memory of his precious death until he comes again.

Hear us, merciful Father, we humbly pray,
and grant that, by the power of your Holy Spirit,
we receiving these gifts of your creation, this bread and this wine,
according to your Son our Saviour Jesus Christ's holy institution,
in remembrance of his death and passion,
may be partakers of his most blessed body and blood;

who, in the same night that he was betrayed,
took bread and gave you thanks;
he broke it and gave it to his disciples, saying:
Take, eat; this is my body which is given for you;
do this in remembrance of me.

In the same way, after supper
he took the cup and gave you thanks;
he gave it to them, saying:
Drink this, all of you;
this is my blood of the new covenant,
which is shed for you and for many for the forgiveness of sins.
Do this, as often as you drink it,
in remembrance of me.

One of these four acclamations is used

[Great is the mystery of faith:]

All **Christ has died:**
Christ is risen:
Christ will come again.

[Praise to you, Lord Jesus:]

Dying you destroyed
our death,
rising you restored our life:
Lord Jesus, come in glory.

[Christ is the bread of life:]

All **When we eat this bread**
and drink this cup,
we proclaim your death,
Lord Jesus,
until you come in glory.

[Jesus Christ is Lord:]

Lord, by your cross and
resurrection
you have set us free.
You are the Saviour of the
world.

The anamnesis: we identify our action now as the fulfilment of Christ's command, linking the Last Supper with the crucifixion and with us as we pray.

We pray that as we share the sacrament of communion we shall receive the benefits of Christ's death, despite our unworthiness.

The prayer ends in praise with *the doxology*...

... to which we all respond 'Amen'.

Therefore, Lord and heavenly Father,
in remembrance of the precious death and passion,
the mighty resurrection and glorious ascension
of your dear Son Jesus Christ,
we offer you through him this our sacrifice of praise
    and thanksgiving.

Grant that by his merits and death,
and through faith in his blood,
we and all your Church may receive forgiveness of our sins
and all other benefits of his passion.
Although we are unworthy, through our manifold sins,
to offer you any sacrifice,
yet we pray that you will accept this
the duty and service that we owe.
Do not weigh our merits, but pardon our offences,
and fill us all who share in this holy communion
with your grace and heavenly blessing;

through Jesus Christ our Lord,
by whom, and with whom, and in whom,
in the unity of the Holy Spirit,
all honour and glory be yours, almighty Father,
for ever and ever.

All **Amen.**

The service continues with the Lord's Prayer on page 37.

Prayer D is a new prayer written for Common Worship.

The Preface: we praise God for his goodness, remembering that although not all fathers are 'good', our heavenly Father is 'good to us all'.

We praise God by telling the story of our salvation in Jesus.

The Sanctus: we join with the song of the angels, recorded in Isaiah's great vision (Isaiah 6:3), and sung in the Temple in Jerusalem. The hymn may be followed by the acclamation of the people of Jerusalem at the entry of Christ to the city on the first Palm Sunday (Matthew 21:9; Mark 11:9–10; Luke 19:38; John 12:13).

We continue praising God, telling the story of Jesus.

The institution narrative: we recall the Last Supper and Jesus's identification of the bread and wine as his body and blood.

Prayer D

The Lord be with you   *(or)*   The Lord is here.
All **and also with you.**   **His Spirit is with us.**

Lift up your hearts.
All **We lift them to the Lord.**

Let us give thanks to the Lord our God.
All **It is right to give thanks and praise.**

Almighty God, good Father to us all,
your face is turned towards your world.
In love you gave us Jesus your Son
to rescue us from sin and death.
Your Word goes out to call us home
    to the city where angels sing your praise.
We join with them in heaven's song:

All **Holy, holy, holy Lord,**
    God of power and might,
    heaven and earth are full of your glory.
    Hosanna in the highest.
    [Blessed is he who comes in the name of the Lord.
    Hosanna in the highest.]

Father of all, we give you thanks
    for every gift that comes from heaven.

To the darkness Jesus came as your light.
With signs of faith and words of hope
he touched untouchables with love and washed the guilty clean.

This is his story.
All **This is our song:**
    Hosanna in the highest.

The crowds came out to see your Son,
    yet at the end they turned on him.
On the night he was betrayed
he came to table with his friends
    to celebrate the freedom of your people.

This is his story.
All **This is our song:**
    Hosanna in the highest.

The anamnesis: we identify our action now as the fulfilment of Christ's command, linking the Last Supper with the crucifixion and with us as we pray.

The epiclesis: we invoke the power of God the Holy Spirit. Compare Luke 24:31,32. The prayer moves from *praise* to *petition*.

The prayer ends in praise with the song from Revelation 5:13.

Jesus blessed you, Father, for the food;
he took bread, gave thanks, broke it and said:
This is my body, given for you all.
Jesus then gave thanks for the wine;
he took the cup, gave it and said:
This is my blood, shed for you all
    for the forgiveness of sins.
Do this in remembrance of me.

This is our story.

All **This is our song:**
Hosanna in the highest.

Therefore, Father, with this bread and this cup
we celebrate the cross
on which he died to set us free.
Defying death he rose again
and is alive with you to plead for us and all the world.

This is our story.

All **This is our song:**
Hosanna in the highest.

Send your Spirit on us now
that by these gifts we may feed on Christ
    with opened eyes and hearts on fire.

May we and all who share this food
offer ourselves to live for you
and be welcomed at your feast in heaven
    where all creation worships you,
Father, Son and Holy Spirit:

All **Blessing and honour and glory and power**
be yours for ever and ever.
Amen.

The service continues with the Lord's Prayer on page 37.

Prayer E is a new prayer written for Common Worship.

The Preface: we praise God for his goodness. These brief words recall Christ's death and resurrection. They may be replaced with a seasonal preface.

The Sanctus: we join with the song of the angels, recorded in Isaiah's great vision (Isaiah 6:3), and sung in the Temple in Jerusalem. The hymn may be followed by the acclamation of the people of Jerusalem at the entry of Christ to the city on the first Palm Sunday (Matthew 21:9; Mark 11:9–10; Luke 19:38; John 12:13).

The epiclesis: we invoke the power of God the Holy Spirit. The prayer moves from praise to petition.

The institution narrative: we recall the Last Supper and Jesus's identification of the bread and wine as his body and blood.

Prayer E

The Lord be with you   *(or)*   The Lord is here.

All **and also with you.**   **His Spirit is with us.**

Lift up your hearts.

All **We lift them to the Lord.**

Let us give thanks to the Lord our God.

All **It is right to give thanks and praise.**

Here follows an extended Preface or the following

Father, you made the world and love your creation.
You gave your Son Jesus Christ to be our Saviour.
His dying and rising have set us free from sin and death.
And so we gladly thank you,
with saints and angels praising you, and *saying:*

All **Holy, holy, holy Lord,**
God of power and might,
heaven and earth are full of your glory.
Hosanna in the highest.
[Blessed is he who comes in the name of the Lord.
Hosanna in the highest.]

We praise and bless you, loving Father,
through Jesus Christ, our Lord;
and as we obey his command,
send your Holy Spirit,
that broken bread and wine outpoured
may be for us the body and blood of your dear Son.

On the night before he died he had supper with his friends
and, taking bread, he praised you.
He broke the bread, gave it to them and said:
Take, eat; this is my body which is given for you;
do this in remembrance of me.

When supper was ended he took the cup of wine.
Again he praised you, gave it to them and said:
Drink this, all of you;
this is my blood of the new covenant,
which is shed for you and for many for the forgiveness of sins.
Do this, as often as you drink it, in remembrance of me.

The *anamnesis*: we identify our action now as the fulfilment of Christ's command, linking the Last Supper with the crucifixion and with us as we pray.

The acclamation 'When we eat this bread...' is from 1 Corinthians 11:26.

We pray that we shall receive the benefits of the sacramental meal, looking forward to the kingdom of God.

The prayer ends in praise with *the doxology*...

... to which we all respond 'Amen'.

So, Father, we remember all that Jesus did,
in him we plead with confidence his sacrifice
    made once for all upon the cross.

Bringing before you the bread of life and cup of salvation,
we proclaim his death and resurrection
until he comes in glory.

One of these four acclamations is used

[Great is the mystery of faith:]

All **Christ has died:**
Christ is risen:
Christ will come again.

[Praise to you, Lord Jesus:]

Dying you destroyed
   our death,
rising you restored our life:
Lord Jesus, come in glory.

[Christ is the bread of life:]

All **When we eat this bread**
   and drink this cup,
we proclaim your death,
   Lord Jesus,
until you come in glory.

[Jesus Christ is Lord:]

Lord, by your cross and
   resurrection
you have set us free.
You are the Saviour of the
   world.

Lord of all life,
help us to work together for that day
when your kingdom comes
and justice and mercy will be seen in all the earth.

Look with favour on your people,
gather us in your loving arms
and bring us with [N *and*] all the saints
to feast at your table in heaven.

Through Christ, and with Christ, and in Christ,
in the unity of the Holy Spirit,
all honour and glory are yours, O loving Father,
for ever and ever.

All **Amen.**

The service continues with the Lord's Prayer on page 37.

Prayer F is much influenced by the Eastern Orthodox prayer attributed to St Basil of Caesarea.

The Preface: we praise God for his goodness.

This preface tells the story of our creation (Genesis 1, 2) and rebellion (Genesis 3) and recalls the struggle throughout the Old Testament to be faithful to God the Father.

The Sanctus: we join with the song of the angels, recorded in Isaiah's great vision (Isaiah 6:3), and sung in the Temple in Jerusalem. The hymn may be followed by the acclamation of the people of Jerusalem at the entry of Christ to the city on the first Palm Sunday (Matthew 21:9; Mark 11:9–10; Luke 19:38; John 12:13).

The prayer continues to praise God, now telling the New Testament story.

Prayer F

The Lord be with you   *(or)*   The Lord is here.
All   **and also with you.**   **His Spirit is with us.**

Lift up your hearts.
All   **We lift them to the Lord.**

Let us give thanks to the Lord our God.
All   **It is right to give thanks and praise.**

You are worthy of our thanks and praise,
Lord God of truth,
for by the breath of your mouth
you have spoken your word,
and all things have come into being.

You fashioned us in your image
and placed us in the garden of your delight.
Though we chose the path of rebellion
you would not abandon your own.

Again and again you drew us into your covenant of grace.
You gave your people the law and taught us by your prophets
to look for your reign of justice, mercy and peace.

As we watch for the signs of your kingdom on earth,
we echo the song of the angels in heaven,
evermore praising you and *saying:*

All   **Holy, holy, holy Lord,**
God of power and might,
heaven and earth are full of your glory.
Hosanna in the highest.
[Blessed is he who comes in the name of the Lord.
Hosanna in the highest.]

Lord God, you are the most holy one,
enthroned in splendour and light,
yet in the coming of your Son Jesus Christ
you reveal the power of your love
made perfect in our human weakness.

[All   **Amen. Lord, we believe.]**

The institution narrative: we recall the Last Supper and Jesus's identification of the bread and wine as his body and blood.

The anamnesis: we identify our action now as the fulfilment of Christ's command, linking the Last Supper with the crucifixion and with us as we pray.

The epiclesis: we invoke the power of God the Holy Spirit. The prayer moves from *praise* to *petition*.

In this acclamation, and the one following, we join in the invocation of the Holy Spirit.

Embracing our humanity,
Jesus showed us the way of salvation;
loving us to the end,
he gave himself to death for us;
dying for his own,
he set us free from the bonds of sin,
that we might rise and reign with him in glory.

[*All* **Amen. Lord, we believe.**]

On the night he gave up himself for us all
he took bread and gave you thanks;
he broke it and gave it to his disciples, saying:
Take, eat; this is my body which is given for you;
do this in remembrance of me.

[*All* **Amen. Lord, we believe.**]

In the same way, after supper
he took the cup and gave you thanks;
he gave it to them, saying:
Drink this, all of you; this is my blood of the new covenant
which is shed for you and for many for the forgiveness of sins.
Do this, as often as you drink it, in remembrance of me.

[*All* **Amen. Lord, we believe.**]

Therefore we proclaim the death that he suffered on the cross,
we celebrate his resurrection, his bursting from the tomb,
we rejoice that he reigns at your right hand on high
and we long for his coming in glory.

[*All* **Amen. Come, Lord Jesus.**]

As we recall the one, perfect sacrifice of our redemption,
Father, by your Holy Spirit let these gifts of your creation
be to us the body and blood of our Lord Jesus Christ;
form us into the likeness of Christ
and make us a perfect offering in your sight.

[*All* **Amen. Come, Holy Spirit.**]

These brief petitions recall Christ's proclamation of the kingdom in Luke 4:16–21, after Isaiah 61:1–2.

Each celebration of the Eucharist is a foretaste of this feast in God's kingdom.

The prayer ends in praise with the doxology...

... to which we all respond 'Amen'.

Look with favour on your people
and in your mercy hear the cry of our hearts.
Bless the earth,
heal the sick,
let the oppressed go free
and fill your Church with power from on high.

[*All* **Amen. Come, Holy Spirit.]**

Gather your people from the ends of the earth
to feast with [N *and*] all your saints
at the table in your kingdom,
where the new creation is brought to perfection
in Jesus Christ our Lord;

by whom, and with whom, and in whom,
in the unity of the Holy Spirit,
all honour and glory be yours, almighty Father,
for ever and ever.

All **Amen.**

The service continues with the Lord's Prayer on page 37.

Prayer G is derived from a prayer written in 1984 and adapted for Common Worship.

The Preface: we praise God for his goodness.

We praise God for his creation: these words echo Psalm 19:1–4. 'Silent music' derives from the writing of John of the Cross (1542–91). As the crown of creation we too glorify God.

The Sanctus: we join with the song of the angels, recorded in Isaiah's great vision (Isaiah 6:3), and sung in the Temple in Jerusalem. The hymn may be followed by the acclamation of the people of Jerusalem at the entry of Christ to the city on the first Palm Sunday (Matthew 21:9; Mark 11:9–10; Luke 19:38; John 12:13).

The prayer continues to praise God, thanking him for remaining faithful to us. These words are reminiscent of Isaiah 66:13, Matthew 23:37, and Luke 13:34.

The prayer turns to the story of God the Son, continuing to praise God, and alluding to John 6:35.

Prayer G

The Lord be with you   *(or)*   The Lord is here.
All   **and also with you.**   **His Spirit is with us.**

Lift up your hearts.
All   **We lift them to the Lord.**

Let us give thanks to the Lord our God.
All   **It is right to give thanks and praise.**

Blessed are you, Lord God,
our light and our salvation;
to you be glory and praise for ever.

From the beginning you have created all things
and all your works echo the silent music of your praise.
In the fullness of time you made us in your image,
the crown of all creation.

You give us breath and speech, that with angels and archangels
and all the powers of heaven
we may find a voice to sing your praise:

All   **Holy, holy, holy Lord,**
God of power and might,
heaven and earth are full of your glory.
Hosanna in the highest.
[Blessed is he who comes in the name of the Lord.
Hosanna in the highest.]

How wonderful the work of your hands, O Lord.
As a mother tenderly gathers her children,
you embraced a people as your own.
When they turned away and rebelled
your love remained steadfast.

From them you raised up Jesus our Saviour, born of Mary,
to be the living bread,
in whom all our hungers are satisfied.

He offered his life for sinners,
and with a love stronger than death
he opened wide his arms on the cross.

The institution narrative: we recall the Last Supper and Jesus's identification of the bread and wine as his body and blood.

This acclamation is from 1 Corinthians 11:26.

On the night before he died,
he came to supper with his friends
and, taking bread, he gave you thanks.
He broke it and gave it to them, saying:
Take, eat; this is my body which is given for you;
do this in remembrance of me.

At the end of supper, taking the cup of wine,
he gave you thanks, and said:
Drink this, all of you; this is my blood of the new covenant,
which is shed for you and for many for the forgiveness of sins.
Do this, as often as you drink it, in remembrance of me.

One of these four acclamations is used

[Great is the mystery of faith:]

All **Christ has died:
Christ is risen:
Christ will come again.**

(or)

[Praise to you, Lord Jesus:]

All **Dying you destroyed our death,
rising you restored our life:
Lord Jesus, come in glory.**

(or)

[Christ is the bread of life:]

All **When we eat this bread and drink this cup,
we proclaim your death, Lord Jesus,
until you come in glory.**

(or)

[Jesus Christ is Lord:]

All **Lord, by your cross and resurrection
you have set us free.
You are the Saviour of the world.**

The anamnesis: we identify our action now as the fulfilment of Christ's command, linking the Last Supper with the crucifixion and with us as we pray.

The epiclesis: we invoke the power of God the Holy Spirit. The prayer moves from *praise* to *petition*.

These words hint at Ephesians 4:13–16 and 2:20–21.

The prayer ends in praise with *the doxology*...

... culminating in the song from Revelation 5:13.

Father, we plead with confidence
his sacrifice made once for all upon the cross;
we remember his dying and rising in glory,
and we rejoice that he intercedes for us at your right hand.

Pour out your Holy Spirit as we bring before you
these gifts of your creation;
may they be for us the body and blood of your dear Son.

As we eat and drink these holy things in your presence,
form us in the likeness of Christ,
and build us into a living temple to your glory.

[Remember, Lord, your Church in every land.
Reveal her unity, guard her faith,
and preserve her in peace ...]

Bring us at the last with [N and] all the saints
to the vision of that eternal splendour
for which you have created us;
through Jesus Christ, our Lord,
by whom, with whom, and in whom,
with all who stand before you in earth and heaven,
we worship you, Father almighty, in songs of everlasting praise:

All **Blessing and honour and glory and power
be yours for ever and ever.
Amen.**

The service continues with the Lord's Prayer on page 37.

Prayer H is a new prayer written for Common Worship.

The Preface: we praise God for his goodness.

'meet us', 'embraced us' – see Luke 15:11–32, especially verse 20, and also the second prayer on page 45.
'sit and eat' – see the poem on page 42.

'live in him and he in us' – see John 6:56 and the prayers on page 43.
'sacrifice for sin' – compare Hebrews 9:26.

The institution narrative: we recall the Last Supper and Jesus's identification of the bread and wine as his body and blood.

'bread of life' – see John 6:35.

'shed for all' – compare Matthew 26:28; Mark 14:24.

Prayer H

The Lord be with you   *(or)*   The Lord is here.
All **and also with you.**   **His Spirit is with us.**

Lift up your hearts.
All **We lift them to the Lord.**

Let us give thanks to the Lord our God.
All **It is right to give thanks and praise.**

It is right to praise you, Father, Lord of all creation;
in your love you made us for yourself.

When we turned away
you did not reject us,
but came to meet us in your Son.
All **You embraced us as your children**
and welcomed us to sit and eat with you.

In Christ you shared our life
that we might live in him and he in us.
All **He opened his arms of love upon the cross**
and made for all the perfect sacrifice for sin.

On the night he was betrayed,
at supper with his friends
he took bread, and gave you thanks;
he broke it and gave it to them, saying:
Take, eat; this is my body which is given for you;
do this in remembrance of me.
All **Father, we do this in remembrance of him:**
his body is the bread of life.

At the end of supper, taking the cup of wine,
he gave you thanks, and said:
Drink this, all of you; this is my blood of the new covenant,
which is shed for you for the forgiveness of sins;
do this in remembrance of me.
All **Father, we do this in remembrance of him:**
his blood is shed for all.

The anamnesis: we identify our action now as the fulfilment of Christ's command, linking the Last Supper with the crucifixion and with us as we pray. Moving from *praise* to *petition*, the prayer continues into *the epiclesis*, in which we invoke the power of God the Holy Spirit.

The prayer ends in praise with the *Sanctus:* we join with the song of the angels, recorded in Isaiah's great vision (Isaiah 6:3), and sung in the Temple in Jerusalem.

As we proclaim his death and celebrate his rising in glory,
send your Holy Spirit that this bread and this wine
may be to us the body and blood of your dear Son.

All **As we eat and drink these holy gifts
make us one in Christ, our risen Lord.**

With your whole Church throughout the world
we offer you this sacrifice of praise
and lift our voice to join the eternal song of heaven:

All **Holy, holy, holy Lord,
God of power and might,
heaven and earth are full of your glory.
Hosanna in the highest.**

The service continues with the Lord's Prayer on page 37.

The Ten Commandments (sometimes called the *Decalogue* from the Hebrew name, the *Ten Words*) are one of the best known and most influential passages of the Bible, often taken to be a general summary of morality. They appear in two different places in the Old Testament. They are the first of the laws given to the people of Israel, described in Exodus 20, when Moses climbs Mount Sinai and returns with the tablets of stone. There is another, slightly longer, version in Deuteronomy 5.

In *Common Worship* the Commandments appear in two versions. The first is a modern translation of the form in the *Book of Common Prayer*. There, the Commandments, in the fuller version of Deuteronomy 5, are printed at the beginning of the Holy Communion service. In the response we acknowledge our failure to keep the commandments and ask for God's help to do better.

Supplementary Texts

¶ *Penitential Material*

The Commandments

I

At the discretion of the minister, responses may be used only after the fourth and tenth Commandments, or only after the tenth Commandment.

God spoke these words and said: I am the Lord your God
[who brought you out of the land of Egypt, out of the house of slavery];
you shall have no other gods but me.

All **Lord, have mercy upon us,
and incline our hearts to keep this law.**

You shall not make for yourself any idol,
whether in the form of anything that is in heaven above,
or that is on the earth beneath, or that is in the water under the earth.
You shall not bow down to them or worship them.
[For I the Lord your God am a jealous God,
punishing children for the iniquity of parents
to the third and the fourth generation of those who reject me,
but showing steadfast love to a thousand generations of those
  who love me
and keep my commandments.]

All **Lord, have mercy upon us,
and incline our hearts to keep this law.**

You shall not take the name of the Lord your God in vain
[for the Lord will not hold him guiltless who takes his name in vain].

All **Lord, have mercy upon us,
and incline our hearts to keep this law.**

Remember the Sabbath day, and keep it holy.
For six days you shall labour and do all your work.
But the seventh day is a Sabbath to the Lord your God.
[You shall not do any work –
you, your son or your daughter,
your slaves, your livestock,
or the foreigner who lives among you.
For in six days the Lord made heaven and earth,
the sea, and all that is in them,
but rested the seventh day;
therefore the Lord blessed the seventh day and consecrated it.]

All **Lord, have mercy upon us,
and incline our hearts to keep this law.**

Honour your father and your mother
[so that your days may be long in the land
that the Lord your God is giving you].

All **Lord, have mercy upon us,
and incline our hearts to keep this law.**

You shall not murder.

All **Lord, have mercy upon us,
and incline our hearts to keep this law.**

You shall not commit adultery.

All **Lord, have mercy upon us,
and incline our hearts to keep this law.**

You shall not steal.

All **Lord, have mercy upon us,
and incline our hearts to keep this law.**

You shall not bear false witness [against your neighbour].

All **Lord, have mercy upon us,
and incline our hearts to keep this law.**

You shall not covet [your neighbour's house;
you shall not covet your neighbour's wife, or slaves, or ox, or donkey,
or anything that belongs to your neighbour].

All **Lord, have mercy upon us,
and write all these your laws in our hearts.**

The second form of the Commandments is short, even shorter than Exodus 20. Each commandment is complemented by a phrase drawn from the New Testament. These help us to meditate on God's will and our personal conduct.

Mark 12:30 (and compare Matthew 22:37 and Luke 10:27)

John 4:24

Hebrews 12:28

Colossians 3:2

1 Peter 2:16,17; Galatians 6:10

Romans 12:18,21

1 Corinthians 6:19

Ephesians 4:28

Ephesians 4:25

Acts 20:35

2

Hear these commandments which God has given to his people,
and examine your hearts.

I am the Lord your God: you shall have no other gods but me.
You shall love the Lord your God with all your heart,
with all your soul, with all your mind, and with all your strength.

All **Amen. Lord, have mercy.**

You shall not make for yourself any idol.
God is spirit, and those who worship him must worship in spirit
    and in truth.

All **Amen. Lord, have mercy.**

You shall not dishonour the name of the Lord your God.
You shall worship him with awe and reverence.

All **Amen. Lord, have mercy.**

Remember the Sabbath and keep it holy.
Christ is risen from the dead: set your minds on things that are
above, not on things that are on the earth.

All **Amen. Lord, have mercy.**

Honour your father and mother.
Live as servants of God; let us work for the good of all,
especially members of the household of faith.

All **Amen. Lord, have mercy.**

You shall not commit murder.
Live peaceably with all; overcome evil with good.

All **Amen. Lord, have mercy.**

You shall not commit adultery.
Know that your body is a temple of the Holy Spirit.

All **Amen. Lord, have mercy.**

You shall not steal.
Be honest in all that you do, and care for those in need.

All **Amen. Lord, have mercy.**

You shall not be a false witness.
Let everyone speak the truth.

All **Amen. Lord, have mercy.**

You shall not covet anything which belongs to your neighbour.
Remember the words of the Lord Jesus:

Romans 13:9,10

This confession addresses God as the creator of light. By his
grace we are created in his image, an image we have marred
by our sins. We have walked in the darkness of ignorance and
sin, but we can be led back to the light of the gospel. Compare
the words of the baptism service: 'May Almighty God deliver
you from the powers of darkness, restore in you the image of
his glory, and lead you in the light and obedience of Christ';
and 'God has delivered us from the dominion of darkness and
has given us a place with the saints in light … shine as a light
in the world to the glory of God the Father.'

This short confession uses simple, direct words with little or
no imagery. Familiar phrases are drawn from the confession in
the Book of Common Prayer Holy Communion service (Common
Worship: Services and Prayers for the Church of England, page 237).

'It is more blessed to give than to receive.'

Love your neighbour as yourself, for love is the fulfilling of the law.

All **Amen. Lord, have mercy.**

For another form of the Commandments and forms of the Comfortable Words and the Beatitudes, see pages 109–113.

Confessions

For other authorized confessions, see pages 123–134 and 277–278 in Common Worship: Services and Prayers for the Church of England.

1

All **Father eternal, giver of light and grace,**
we have sinned against you and against our neighbour,
in what we have thought,
in what we have said and done,
through ignorance, through weakness,
through our own deliberate fault.
We have wounded your love,
and marred your image in us.
We are sorry and ashamed,
and repent of all our sins.
For the sake of your Son Jesus Christ,
who died for us,
forgive us all that is past;
and lead us out from darkness
to walk as children of light.
Amen.

2

All **Almighty God, our heavenly Father,**
we have sinned against you,
through our own fault,
in thought, and word, and deed,
and in what we have left undone.
We are heartily sorry,
and repent of all our sins.
For your Son our Lord Jesus Christ's sake,
forgive us all that is past;
and grant that we may serve you in newness of life
to the glory of your name.
Amen.

The Apostles' Creed originated as a statement of faith made by those being baptized, and it is used in this way in *Common Worship* (*Common Worship: Services and Prayers for the Church of England*, page 356). The three paragraphs of the creed are linked to the threefold pouring or immersion in water at baptism.

In this creed we each briefly affirm our adherence to the historical facts and beliefs of the Christian faith. This reflects the declaration and promises made at our baptism, when we became members of the Church, the body of Christ.

¶ The Apostles' Creed

The origin of the Apostles' Creed is the profession of faith made at baptism. This association may have implications for the occasion when it is used at Holy Communion.

All **I believe in God, the Father almighty,
creator of heaven and earth.**

**I believe in Jesus Christ, his only Son, our Lord,
who was conceived by the Holy Spirit,
born of the Virgin Mary,
suffered under Pontius Pilate,
was crucified, died, and was buried;
he descended to the dead.
On the third day he rose again;
he ascended into heaven,
he is seated at the right hand of the Father,
and he will come to judge the living and the dead.**

**I believe in the Holy Spirit,
the holy catholic Church,
the communion of saints,
the forgiveness of sins,
the resurrection of the body,
and the life everlasting.
Amen.**

For other forms of the Creeds and authorized Affirmations of Faith, see pages 139–152 in Common Worship: Services and Prayers for the Church of England.

These prayers may be used at the Preparation of the Table (see page 31). There are more prayers on pages 291–293 of *Common Worship: Services and Prayers for the Church of England*, which are worth further study.

In 1 Chronicles 29:11,14 King David gathered together the offerings of Israel with which to build the Temple at Jerusalem, giving thanks and praising God in these words.

In very simple words this prayer points to what we shall be doing in the eucharistic prayer that follows. This prayer might be used when the bread has been baked by members of the congregation, when children are being admitted to communion at the service, or where the service has been organized with the needs or offerings of children particularly in mind.

There are several prayers, each beginning 'Blessed are you, Lord God', which give thanks to God for his gifts to us. They follow the pattern of Jewish prayers said at table when bread and wine are taken or candles lit. Perhaps this form was familiar in the time of Jesus. Our response is to praise God for his goodness.

¶ *Prayers at the Preparation of the Table*

Yours, Lord, is the greatness, the power,
the glory, the splendour, and the majesty;
for everything in heaven and on earth is yours.

All   **All things come from you,
and of your own do we give you.**

*In the following prayer, the texts for single voice need not be spoken
by the president. It will sometimes be appropriate to ask children
to speak them.*

With this bread that we bring

All   **we shall remember Jesus.**

With this wine that we bring

All   **we shall remember Jesus.**

Bread for his body,
wine for his blood,
gifts from God to his table we bring.

All   **We shall remember Jesus.**

For further prayers, see pages 291–293 in Common Worship:
Services and Prayers for the Church of England.

The response to prayers which begin 'Blessed…' is
Blessed be God for ever.

These prayers may be used instead of those on page 45. They are testimony to the significance of ecumenical friendship. The first prayer is taken from the 1975 *Methodist Service Book* and the third is adapted from the *Book of Common Order* of the Church of Scotland. The second prayer links the two great sacraments, baptism and holy communion, praying that God will renew his baptized people in his service.

Together with the prayers on pages 45 and 116–118, these may also be used for private thanks and devotion after receiving the sacrament.

¶ Prayers after Communion

1

All **We thank you, Lord,**
that you have fed us in this sacrament,
united us with Christ,
and given us a foretaste of the heavenly banquet
prepared for all peoples.
Amen.

2

All **Faithful God,**
in baptism you have adopted us as your children,
made us members of the body of Christ
and chosen us as inheritors of your kingdom:
we thank you that in this Eucharist
you renew your promises within us,
empower us by your Spirit to witness and to serve,
and send us out as disciples of your Son,
Jesus Christ our Lord.
Amen.

3

All **You have opened to us the Scriptures, O Christ,**
and you have made yourself known
in the breaking of the bread.
Abide with us, we pray,
that, blessed by your royal presence,
we may walk with you
all the days of our life,
and at its end behold you
in the glory of the eternal Trinity,
one God for ever and ever.
Amen.

For Post Communions, see pages 298 and 375–447 in
Common Worship: Services and Prayers for the Church of England.

The notes to the Holy Communion service in *Common Worship: Services and Prayers for the Church of England* encourage 'careful devotional preparation' for every communicant. This form of preparation may be used publicly or privately, or other forms may be used.

Preparation will include thinking about what we have done wrong and a form for the Examination of Conscience is provided on pages 112, 114. We may need to put right things which have arisen with others. Preparation may also include thinking about God's gifts to us, especially his gift of himself, his death on the cross for our sake and his resurrection, and his gift of the sacrament of communion in which we mystically share his body and blood. The Exhortation (page 109) and the Comfortable Words (page 111) remind us of this.

This Preparation begins in prayer for the Holy Spirit and the sevenfold gifts of the Spirit listed in Isaiah 11:2 – wisdom and understanding, counsel and inward strength, knowledge and true godliness, and delight in the fear of the Lord.

This early mediaeval hymn, translated by Bishop John Cosin (1594–1672), is traditionally sung at the ordination of priests and bishops.

A Form of Preparation

This form may be used in any of three ways.

It may be used by individuals as part of their preparation for Holy Communion.

It may be used corporately on suitable occasions within Holy Communion where it replaces the sections entitled 'Prayer of Preparation' and 'Prayers of Penitence'.

It may be used as a separate service of preparation. When used in this way, there should be added at the beginning a greeting and at the end the Peace and the Lord's Prayer. Hymns, psalms and other suitable liturgical material may also be included.

Come, Holy Ghost *(Veni creator Spiritus)*

All   Come, Holy Ghost, our souls inspire,
And lighten with celestial fire;
Thou the anointing Spirit art,
Who dost thy sevenfold gifts impart.

Thy blessed unction from above
Is comfort, life and fire of love;
Enable with perpetual light
The dullness of our blinded sight.

Anoint and cheer our soiled face
With the abundance of thy grace;
Keep far our foes, give peace at home;
Where thou art guide no ill can come.

Teach us to know the Father, Son,
And thee, of Both, to be but One;
That through the ages all along
This may be our endless song:

Praise to thy eternal merit,
Father, Son and Holy Spirit.
Amen.

The Ten Commandments: see pages 92, 96. Here the Commandments are in the same brief form as on page 97, but without the additional sentences from the New Testament.

Exhortation

As we gather at the Lord's table we must recall the promises and
warnings given to us in the Scriptures and so examine ourselves and
repent of our sins. We should give thanks to God for his redemption
of the world through his Son Jesus Christ and, as we remember
Christ's death for us and receive the pledge of his love, resolve
to serve him in holiness and righteousness all the days of our life.

The Commandments

Hear the commandments which God has given to his people,
and examine your hearts.

I am the Lord your God: you shall have no other gods but me.

All   **Amen. Lord, have mercy.**

You shall not make for yourself any idol.

All   **Amen. Lord, have mercy.**

You shall not dishonour the name of the Lord your God.

All   **Amen. Lord, have mercy.**

Remember the Sabbath and keep it holy.

All   **Amen. Lord, have mercy.**

Honour your father and your mother.

All   **Amen. Lord, have mercy.**

You shall not commit murder.

All   **Amen. Lord, have mercy.**

You shall not commit adultery.

All   **Amen. Lord, have mercy.**

You shall not steal.

All   **Amen. Lord, have mercy.**

You shall not bear false witness against your neighbour.

All   **Amen. Lord, have mercy.**

You shall not covet anything which belongs to your neighbour.

All   **Amen. Lord, have mercy upon us
    and write all these your laws in our hearts.**

This summary is from Mark 12:29–31; compare Matthew 22:37–40 and Luke 10:25–28. Jesus gave this response to a question about the Commandments of the Old Testament and added that the questioner, who understood this, was close to the kingdom of God.

These sentences of scripture express God's love for us. They are a source from which we may draw strength and solace.

Or one of the forms of the Commandments in the Supplementary Texts (pages 93–99) may be used.

Or, in place of the Commandments, one of these texts may be used.

Summary of the Law

Our Lord Jesus Christ said:
The first commandment is this:
'Hear, O Israel, the Lord our God is the only Lord.
You shall love the Lord your God with all your heart,
with all your soul, with all your mind,
and with all your strength.'

The second is this: 'Love your neighbour as yourself.'
There is no other commandment greater than these.
On these two commandments hang all the law and the prophets.

All **Amen. Lord, have mercy.**

(or)

The Comfortable Words

Hear the words of comfort our Saviour Christ says
to all who truly turn to him:

Come to me, all who labour and are heavy laden,
and I will give you rest.   *Matthew 11.28*

God so loved the world that he gave his only-begotten Son,
that whoever believes in him should not perish
but have eternal life.   *John 3.16*

Hear what Saint Paul says:
This saying is true, and worthy of full acceptance,
that Christ Jesus came into the world to save sinners.   *I Timothy 1.15*

Hear what Saint John says:
If anyone sins, we have an advocate with the Father,
Jesus Christ the righteous;
and he is the propitiation for our sins.   *I John 2.1, 2*

(or)

The Beatitudes are at the heart of Jesus's teaching at the Sermon on the Mount, Matthew 5,6,7. Similar teaching is given at Luke 6:20–22.

An Examination of Conscience

An essential part of preparing for the Eucharist is to examine our conscience, and be reconciled with God and our neighbour. The following questions may be of help in considering where we have fallen short.

Love of God

You shall love the Lord your God with all your heart, with all your soul, and with all your mind, and with all your strength. Mark 12:30

Do I love God?
Do I make an idol of money, possessions or sex?
Do I blaspheme by taking the name of the Lord
    in vain?
Do I study and listen to the Word of God and try to
    obey God's commandments?
Do I go to church regularly on Sundays and
    holy days?
Do I keep Sunday as a holy day?
Do I say my prayers regularly?

Love of Neighbour

Love your neighbour as yourself. Mark 12:31

Have I hated others?
Do I love my family and friends?
Have I been faithful to my spouse?
Have I been kind and helpful to my children?
Have I honoured my mother and my father?
Do I contribute my share to the Church?
Do I contribute generously to good causes?

Have I lived up to the commission I received at my
    baptism and confirmation?
Am I a peacemaker and an example to others of
    Christian living?

The Beatitudes

Let us hear our Lord's blessing on those who follow him.

Blessed are the poor in spirit,
for theirs is the kingdom of heaven.

Blessed are those who mourn,
for they shall be comforted.

Blessed are the meek,
for they shall inherit the earth.

Blessed are those who hunger and thirst after righteousness,
for they shall be satisfied.

Blessed are the merciful,
for they shall obtain mercy.

Blessed are the pure in heart,
for they shall see God.

Blessed are the peacemakers,
for they shall be called children of God.

Blessed are those who suffer persecution for righteousness' sake,
for theirs is the kingdom of heaven.

Silence for Reflection

Do I keep my conscience in good repair?

Do I hunger and thirst for righteousness and speak up for my beliefs and principles?

Have I respected the integrity of creation – animals and natural resources?

Do I encourage my family and children to live a Christian life?

Do I visit the bereaved and the lonely, the sick and the imprisoned?

Have I stolen from others?

Have I cheated my spouse, my employer, my employee or others?

Have I made restitution of what I have stolen?

Have I damaged others' good name?

Have I been quarrelsome?

Have I thought ill of others and used others for my own ends?

Have I exploited others sexually?

The Way of Perfection

Be perfect as your heavenly Father is perfect.   Matthew 5:48

Do I fast and practise self-control?

Have I followed what my conscience tells me?

Have I tried to acquire habits of wisdom and understanding?

Have I wallowed in self-pity?

Have I allowed myself to be consumed by ambition, bitterness or disappointment?

Have I wasted money?

Have I kept my word?

Have I been proud?

Have I coveted other people's possessions or spouse?

Have I indulged impurity?

Have I been envious of others?

Have I been greedy?

Have I been angry?

Have I been lazy?

Andrew Burnham

Confession

All **Father eternal, giver of light and grace,**
we have sinned against you and against our neighbour,
in what we have thought,
in what we have said and done,
through ignorance, through weakness,
through our own deliberate fault.
We have wounded your love
and marred your image in us.
We are sorry and ashamed
and repent of all our sins.
For the sake of your Son Jesus Christ,
who died for us,
forgive us all that is past
and lead us out from darkness
to walk as children of light.
Amen.

Or another authorized confession may be used.

Absolution

Almighty God, our heavenly Father,
who in his great mercy
has promised forgiveness of sins
to all those who with heartfelt repentance and true faith
  turn to him:
have mercy on *you*;
pardon and deliver *you* from all *your* sins;
confirm and strengthen *you* in all goodness;
and bring *you* to everlasting life;
through Jesus Christ our Lord.

All **Amen.**

Prayers and Meditations

These prayers and meditations may be helpful before and after receiving the sacrament. Other suitable prayers will be found on pages 42, 43 (before receiving), and pages 45, 105 (after receiving). The words of many communion hymns are also appropriate.

Other suitable prayers will be found on pages 42, 43 (before receiving), and pages 45, 105 (after receiving).

Before receiving communion

Lord, I acknowledge that I am far from worthy
to approach and touch this sacrament.
But I trust in that mercy
which caused you to lay down your life for sinners,
that they might be saved from sin.
So I, a sinner, presume to receive these gifts.
Make me, O Lord, so to receive with lips and heart
and know by faith and love,
that by virtue of this sacrament
I may die to sin as you died,
and rise to fullness of life as you rose.
May I be made worthy
to become a member of your holy body,
a stone in your living temple,
and let me rejoice forever
in your eternal love.

> *Anselm of Canterbury* (1033–1109)

After receiving communion

Author of life divine
who hast a table spread,
furnished with mystic wine
and everlasting bread,
preserve the life thyself hast given,
and feed and train us up for heaven.

Our needy souls sustain
with fresh supplies of love,
till all thy life we gain,
and all thy fullness prove,
and, strengthened by thy perfect grace,
behold without a veil thy face.

> *Charles Wesley* (1707–88)

Bread of the world, in mercy broken,
Wine of the soul, in mercy shed,
by whom the words of life were spoken,
and in whose death our sins are dead:
look on the heart by sorrow broken,
look on the tears by sinners shed;
and be thy feast to us the token
that by thy grace our souls are fed
                    Reginald Heber (1783–1826)

Father in heaven,
whose Church on earth is a sign of your heavenly peace,
an image of the new and eternal Jerusalem:
grant to us in the days of our pilgrimage
that, fed with the living bread of heaven,
and united in the body of your Son,
we may be the temple of your presence,
the place of your glory on earth,
and a sign of your peace in the world;
through Jesus Christ our Lord. Amen.
          Common Worship: Services and Prayers for the Church
          of England page 446

Holy and blessed God,
you have fed us with the body and blood of your Son
and filled us with your Holy Spirit:
may we honour you,
not only with our lips
but in lives dedicated to the service
    of Jesus Christ our Lord. Amen.
          Common Worship: Services and Prayers for the Church
          of England page 420

Living God,
your Son made himself known to his disciples
in the breaking of bread:
open the eyes of our faith,
that we may see him in all his redeeming work;
who is alive and reigns, now and for ever. Amen.
          Common Worship: Services and Prayers for the Church
          of England page 401

Soul of Christ, sanctify me,
Body of Christ, save me,
Blood of Christ, inebriate me,
Water from the side of Christ, wash me,
Passion of Christ, strengthen me.
O good Jesus, hear me.
Within your wounds hide me.
Let me not be separated from you,
from the malicious enemy, defend me,
in the hour of my death call me
and bid me come to you,
that with your saints I may praise you
for ever and ever. Amen
Latin, fourteenth century

This is the hour of banquet and of song;
this is the heavenly table spread for me;
here let me feast, and feasting still prolong
the hallowed hour of fellowship with thee.

Too soon we rise; we go our several ways;
the feast, though not the love, is past and gone,
the bread and wine consumed: yet all our days
thou still art here with us, our shield and sun.

Feast after feast thus comes and passes by,
yet, passing, points to the glad feast above,
giving sweet foretaste of the festal joy,
the Lamb's great bridal feast of bliss and love.
Horatius Bonar (1808–89)

You, Lord, are the bread of life and the well of holiness.
Just as you feed me day by day
with the food that sustains my body,
keeping me alive on earth,
I pray that you will feed my soul
with the spiritual bread of eternity,
making me ready for heaven.
Just as you satisfy my bodily thirst
with cool water from the rivers and streams,
I pray that you will pour the water of holiness
    into my soul,
making my every word and deed
a joyful sign of your love.
Basil of Caesarea (c.330–379)

Part Two

Part Two

1 Down the Ages: the History of the Eucharist

For almost two thousand years Christians have been celebrating the Eucharist. In groups large and small, in settings formal and informal, with ceremonial complex and simple, Christians have followed the command to 'do this in remembrance of me'.

The New Testament records that the Last Supper took place at the time of Passover, and includes several other meals which are suggestive of the Eucharist. These include the feedings of the multitudes (Matthew 14:15–21; Mark 6:34–44 and 8:1–9; Luke 9:12–17; John 6:1–13), and several of the resurrection appearances, especially that at Emmaus in Luke 24:13–32, where the disciples recognised Jesus in the breaking of bread. Some other appearances are also at meals. In 1 Corinthians 11:23–25, Paul tells of the tradition which had been handed on to him, of remembrance in the context of a communal meal.

The Early Church and the Middle Ages

Persecution followed, and gatherings of Christians became difficult, and in time the meal became a ritual meal. By the mid-second century, this ritual meal was preceded by Bible readings and prayers and the kiss of peace, a structure recognisable today. The bread and the cup were now treated equally in the ritual, just as they are today. There are records elsewhere of the Eucharist: the Roman governor Pliny the Younger wrote that it was reported that Christians ate human flesh and blood. Gradually the form of the service became more settled: by the third century in Rome we have a sample eucharistic prayer which is recognisable today. Indeed, Prayer B in this service is closely based on it, and so, to a lesser extent, is Prayer A.

In 313 the Emperor Constantine ended the persecution of Christianity, and it was possible for the Eucharist to become a public event. The local church would gather in each city around its bishop to celebrate the Eucharist together. The service became more elaborate as ceremonial spread from the imperial court to the major cities. The ritual led to a greater emphasis on awe and adoration and eventually people received the sacrament much less frequently. As Christianity spread, the service was led by priests in the towns and villages, since the bishop could not be at every service, although the celebration around the bishop remained the ideal.

By the Middle Ages, most of the western Church had adopted the Latin language rite used in Rome – the Roman Rite – though there were many local variations or 'uses'. Theologians such as Thomas Aquinas tried to explain in what way the sacrament was the body and blood of Christ. Increasingly, people came to believe that the Eucharist, identified with the saving sacrifice of Christ on the cross, was able to reduce the time spent by the dead in purgatory. Wealthy people endowed chapels in which priests could say the mass each day for the repose of their souls. For the ordinary faithful it was enough that they were present and able to venerate the sacrament, which by now was generally only consumed by the priest. Even when they did make their communion, the cup was not offered them, and the service in Latin was understood only by the educated few. These and other practices were ripe for reform. The Reformation had many causes and effects, but revision of the mass was a high priority. Luther, Calvin and others had different views on the theology of the mass, and each radically simplified the service, translating it out of Latin.

The Reformation

In England, the Church was reformed from within, and Archbishop Cranmer introduced the first *Book of Common Prayer* in 1549, putting the service into English. A second version in 1552 introduced many more changes, and there were various minor revisions in England down to 1662. There was also a Scottish variant which was later adapted elsewhere in the growing Anglican Communion (as it became known), and was a reminder that the service of Holy Communion could have more than one form.

Cranmer's aim was to re-establish Holy Communion as the usual weekly service of the Church, and for all the faithful to receive the sacrament. In this he failed, and in most of the English Church Morning Prayer (often called *mattins*) became the usual Sunday morning service. Holy Communion might only be celebrated monthly or quarterly, and at Easter and Christmas. John Wesley preached the need for regular celebrations but things only started to change under the influence of the Oxford Movement from the 1830s. Its leaders

– John Keble, Edward Pusey and John Henry Newman –
emphasised greater devotion to the sacrament and a more
frequent and richer form of celebration.

Recent Revision

From the start of the twentieth century there were moves for
further liturgical reform. In the Roman Catholic Church, small
groups urged a need for simplification and for all the faithful
to receive the sacrament of Holy Communion regularly. At the
same time, in the Church of England 'parish communion'
gradually became widespread as the main Sunday morning
service. There was an attempt to revise the prayer book in the
1920s, but the proposals were criticised and not authorized.
Only after the Second World War, in the 1960s and 1970s,
did revision finally take place. The Church of England and the
Roman Catholics both produced new English-language services
at about the same time, and the structure of the Eucharist is
seen to be identical in both Churches. Even the language is
identical at many points, as these Churches, along with
Methodists, Baptists, the United Reformed Church and other
English-speaking Churches around the world, worked together
to provide common translations of common prayers. The
1990s saw a further revision, culminating in the publication of
Common Worship in 2000.

And so at the start of the twenty-first century, it is still true
that Christians, week by week and day by day, come together
to celebrate the Eucharist, obeying the instruction of Christ to
'do this in remembrance of me'.

2 Structure, Variety: the Shape of the Eucharist

At first glance the Eucharist can seem a complicated service,
without any particular pattern. In addition there is a large
range of options and choices available in the *Common Worship*
books – a variety which might be bewildering.

There is, however, a simple structure to the service, and
whatever options are chosen, whatever the seasonal variety,
this structure remains.

Order One falls into four sections: the *Gathering*; the *Liturgy
of the Word*; the *Liturgy of the Sacrament*; and the *Dismissal*. This

sequence provides a simple outline in which worshippers come together, hear the Word of God proclaimed in Scripture and preaching, share in the sacrament of communion, and return to their ordinary lives in the light of that eucharistic experience. Within each section there are several elements, all of them important to the development and progress of the total act of worship.

The Gathering

At the start of the service the president greets the people, welcoming us into the action and calling for our attention. We are invited to prepare for worship, perhaps by calling upon God in the words of the Collect for Purity, and by confessing our sins and receiving the assurance of God's forgiveness. We may sing together, perhaps an opening hymn, and perhaps the Gloria. The short prayer called the collect relates to the season or to the particular concerns of a special day, and offers a focus for our petitions at the conclusion of this section.

The Liturgy of the Word

All of this helps us to come together as a community, ready to hear the Word of God proclaimed in the readings, the gospel, and the sermon. In the creed we stand with Christians down the ages in proclaiming our belief in God, Father, Son and Holy Spirit. In the Prayers of Intercession we respond in a different way, looking outward to the needs of the church community and to the world in which it is set, trusting that God hears us when we pray in faith.

The Liturgy of the Sacrament

The Liturgy of the Sacrament is normally introduced by the Peace. This reminds those who have gathered that we must be committed to loving one another in Christ. That peace and love are built up by the gifts of God for which we will give thanks and pray in the eucharistic prayer, and as we receive together the sacrament of communion.

The bread and wine are prepared next, sometimes with extra prayers that honour God for the gifts of the earth. Then comes the eucharistic prayer and the distribution of the communion: these together form the heart of the service. In the prayer we give thanks to God the Father for all that he has done for us, especially in the life, death and resurrection of

Jesus, God the Son, and we pray for the gifts of God the Holy Spirit. The various eucharistic prayers express this in different ways, but in each we pray that the bread and wine may be transformed from the ordinary to the extraordinary, that we may share in the body and blood of Christ. The breaking of the bread is an eloquent symbol of Christ's broken body on the cross; a reminder of the brokenness of our own lives, and the disparate nature of our communities, all of which are capable of being gathered into the love of God. After the communion, a short prayer concludes the Liturgy of the Sacrament.

The Dismissal

It remains for the president to pray for God's blessing on the people and to send us out, in the light of the action in which we have participated. Whether we are told to 'Go in peace to love and serve the Lord', or to 'Go in the peace of Christ', the instruction is to live out the Eucharist in our daily lives.

This simple structure helps us to find our way around the service. Thanks to the liturgical research and reform undertaken in the twentieth century, this structure is found across a range of Christian denominations. If we attend a celebration of the Eucharist in a church of almost any of the western denominations we may not understand the language that is used. However, if we are aware of the direction and structure of the service, we know what is happening and can even participate to some extent. Once we are familiar with the structure, then we can also see how various options fit together, and we are helped to find our way through the service, even in an unfamiliar setting, or with unfamiliar words.

Variety

This variety is expressed in several different ways. First, there is variety across the year, in which particular forms are used in the different seasons of the Church's year. For example, there may be a more penitential form in Lent, or a celebratory form at Easter and at Christmas, or on some saints' days. This variety can help us to feel the changing seasons, just as we experience similar seasonal variety in our everyday lives.

Secondly, most sections of the service offer alternative forms of words. For example, the words of the confession, the gospel acclamation, the introduction to the Peace, the invitation to communion, and the blessing may all be varied. There are eight eucharistic prayers, which between them express a great breadth of understanding of the sacrament. They are written in a range of styles, some of them drawing on ancient tradition, from east and west, others newly-written in simple words. And there are many extra 'proper prefaces' which can be included in some of the eucharistic prayers to mark a season or to celebrate a festival.

Some communities will wish to use a lot of variety, and others will prefer as little variety as possible. The Eucharist in *Common Worship* allows each worshipping community to make its own decisions about this. This will depend on the community's history and worshipping tradition, the availability of different musical resources, the shape of the building and many other factors.

Within this variety, the common structure – the *Gathering*, the *Liturgy of the Word*, the *Liturgy of the Sacrament*, the *Dismissal* – helps to provide a pattern and rhythm to our worship, so that we can return as confident participants in the Eucharist again and again.

3 Decently and in Order: Ways of Celebrating

Was ever another command so obeyed? For century after century, spreading slowly to every continent and country and among every race on earth, this action has been done, in every conceivable human circumstance, for every conceivable human need from infancy and before it to extreme old age and after it, from pinnacles of earthly greatness to the refuge of fugitives in the caves and dens of the earth…

So wrote Dom Gregory Dix of the command to 'do this in remembrance of me'. This celebrated passage, which goes on to describe a host of life circumstances, extreme and everyday, in which the Eucharist has been celebrated, is from his famous book *The Shape of the Liturgy*. Each of us, too, will have our own experiences of its celebration and there will be more to come. Different styles of celebration are appropriate for different occasions. A magnificent service in a grand building with rich hangings and vestments may remind us of the grandeur of

God. A quiet circle around a hospital bed brings more readily to mind the compassion of the God whose Son suffered and died for us and whose presence is made a simple reality, to meet our deepest need, in bread and wine. The Eucharist is celebrated in so many styles in many different places: in churches of all shapes and sizes, in school halls and community centres, in homes, maybe even in gardens, on the road side during pilgrimage, in a sports stadium when thousands gather. Each will provide echoes of the scriptures: perhaps in a home or gathered in a circle in a small church service, we may think of the Last Supper; beside the road we may recall Jesus breaking the bread on arrival at Emmaus; in a sports stadium we may be reminded of the feeding of the five thousand.

Music and Singing

Place is by no means the only variable. We often sing: indeed it is said that the one who sings prays twice. Music used in eucharistic celebrations will be very varied, reflecting the nature of the community at worship. The music may be simple unaccompanied singing in a remote village church, or the plainsong of a religious community, an orchestral mass sung by a professional choir on a great occasion, or guitars in a music group. Each enables the celebrating community to join with the angels and archangels in their song of everlasting praise.

Participation

People will participate in different ways also. On occasion, perhaps at a quiet early morning service with few communicants, or at a time of great need when a few people gather, perhaps in great distress, the president will be responsible for everything. But it is important to remember that at the Eucharist we are all celebrants and we can all, whatever our age or status, offer our gifts and abilities. Some will sing, or read from the Bible, or lead the prayers of the people. Some may welcome the congregation, some may teach the children. Some people may feel themselves to be much quieter and prefer a less conspicuous task, but the ministry of sitting beside a newcomer or stranger, or of sitting with a parent who brings several children to worship, and helping them through, is just as important and its value should never be overlooked.

4 Eucharistic Community, Personal Devotion

As we have seen in Chapter 1 *Down the Ages: the History of the Eucharist*, page 121, Christians have from the earliest times gathered regularly to celebrate the Eucharist together. Often this has been week by week, sometimes day by day, sometimes month by month, but, however frequent, the Eucharist is something we celebrate together. Although there have been exceptions at times, the Eucharist is a communal celebration.

Indeed, it is essentially the principal communal celebration of Christians, and each group of Christians can claim to be the eucharistic community in their town or village or district. And a diocese is formed as the eucharistic community of the Christians in the area, with the bishop at its head. This eucharistic community is itself the body of Christ.

In the Eucharist we are nourished for the work of mission and for our everyday lives. The Eucharist has also been seen by many almost as an act of private devotion, in which an individual prays quietly before the service, 'makes his or her communion', prays quietly after the service, and then leaves. Private devotional practice is indeed important for the Christian, strengthening us for our daily activities, setting our minds at rest, and helping us focus on God, his presence in the service and in our lives, and trying to discern what he would have us do. But the Eucharist is more than this, and we cannot receive all its benefits if we do not understand that it is also a communal experience.

Communal Action

This theme of communal action runs right through the service. From the opening prayer ('cleanse the thoughts of *our* hearts') and the confession ('*we* have sinned against you' and '*we* confess'), the Gloria ('*we* worship you, *we* give you thanks'), the collect ('Let *us* pray'), the creed ('*We* believe'), the intercessions ('hear *our* prayer'), to the eucharistic prayer ('Lift up your hearts', '*We* lift them to the Lord') and the Lord's Prayer ('*Our* Father'), the Prayer of Humble Access ('*We* do not presume'), and on to the prayers after communion ('*we* thank you for feeding us' and '*we* give you thanks and praise'), prayer and praise and statement of faith are seen as a group activity not something we do as individuals.

Nowhere is this more explicit than in the words which accompany the breaking of the bread after the eucharistic prayer. When the president says, 'We break this bread to share in the body of Christ,' the congregation responds, 'Though we are many we are one body, because we all share in one bread.' These words are from Paul's first letter to the Corinthians (1 Corinthians 10:16–17). The Church at Corinth was evidently split into factions and Paul's letter is an extended plea to the Christians there that they should truly worship together and care for one another as a community.

Worshipping Together

The service is about actions as much as words. It is by acting together – worshipping and praying together – that we bring the community into being. Despite our failings, both as individuals and as a group, we build and nourish the body of Christ in this way.

The first part of the service, the Gathering, brings us together to re-form the community from the individuals who are present. The president greets us all and we respond, acknowledging our common purpose. Usually, we then confess together our sins: first, the sins we each as individuals have committed. And, secondly, we confess the sins that we have shared in as a community, the sins that by our action and inaction we are part of: violence and hatred in our town or village; unjust discrimination against groups and individuals; war, famine and preventable disease in lands far off and near at hand; and many others. All these we collectively bring to God seeking his forgiveness, and praying that as individuals and as a community we may do better in the service of Christ.

Often we will sing together, perhaps an opening hymn or song, and on Sundays and holy days outside Advent and Lent the Gloria, a hymn of praise to God. After these introductory parts of the service the president leads the community in prayer, saying the collect of the day. Once we have been gathered, the heart of the service follows in two sections: the Liturgy of the Word and the Liturgy of the Sacrament. The service ends with the brief Dismissal, sending us out, enriched and empowered by Word and Sacrament, to live the life of the kingdom of God, as Christ's own missionaries in the world.

In the Eucharist, God in Christ becomes present for us in a very real way. First, in the reading of the Word of God, particularly in the proclamation of the gospel of Christ. This is why we stand and turn to face the gospel reader, and why the reading often takes place from the midst of the congregation, accompanied by a special acclamation and other ceremonies (see page 24). And secondly, we recognise Christ as present in the breaking of bread, just as did the two disciples on the road to Emmaus on that first Easter Day (Luke 24:30−31). They too had felt his presence in the interpretation of the scriptures, but only recognised it when he took and blessed bread, broke it and shared it with them.

Personal Devotion

This presence of Christ is at the heart of personal devotion in the Eucharist. We adore Christ, whose cross and passion redeemed the world. The sacrament, identified with that cross and that passion (see Chapter 11 *Remembrance and Sacrifice: the Eucharistic Prayer*, page 145) is a great gift from God to his people. In the sacrament we receive the body and blood of Christ, an act of great personal meaning. Yet, in that very act, we are together the body of Christ, and we stand with our fellow Christians across the world, and down the ages, from the time of the Apostles, back to the Last Supper itself.

Personal devotion allows us to concentrate on the service, to set aside for a time the cares of the world, laying them at the foot of the cross. In our devotion we remember our own unworthiness, and the grace of God, freely given, by which alone we are made whole. It allows us to think and to meditate on the love of God, revealed in Christ Jesus. It gives us space to see beyond the words of familiar hymns and prayers and to catch a glimpse of the reign of God, of the banquet in the kingdom of God, of which the Eucharist is but a foretaste.

Above all, personal devotion frees us to concentrate our minds wholly on the service. Often we will be distracted by other people, distracted by boredom or annoyance or by illness or pain, or by a sermon or a hymn we dislike, and much more. It is personal devotion which will help us to overcome these difficulties of human life. This personal devotion involves preparing for the service. *Common Worship* provides a form of preparation which may be used publicly or privately, and *Come to the Feast* adds to this a set of questions that can be used to examine our conscience as we prepare (pages 112, 114).

Personal devotion might also include silent prayer and meditation immediately before the service: the Collect for Purity at the top of page 17 is particularly appropriate if not used at the service. We can also pray silently and meditate after the readings and during the distribution of the communion. *Common Worship* provides several prayers which can be used privately if not used in the service, and *Come to the Feast* adds others. In addition the words of many communion hymns are appropriate. Although we frequently add further devotions after the service, *Common Worship* encourages us to go out immediately the service ends.

Personal devotion might include bowing our heads at the name of Jesus as an acknowledgment that Jesus is Lord, and a reminder of the hymn of praise in Paul's letter to the Philippians (Philippians 2:6–11, especially verse 10). And personal devotion might in some traditions include signing oneself with the sign of the cross as a remembrance of the victory of the cross over death and sin. Personal devotion, in short, enables us to focus on the service and to take our place in the eucharistic community.

Playing Our Part

In this eucharistic community we each have our part to play. Some are ministers, that is *servants*. The president has a special place: as one who is ordained and authorized by the bishop, the president assures us that our local community is part of the wider Church. Similarly the bishop links us with the Church across the country and the world, and as the successor of many earlier bishops also links us with the apostolic Church.

But each person who has an individual role on any occasion is a minister too, some ordained, and some lay. Those who read, or preach, or lead the intercessions, those who bring forward the bread and wine, and the offerings of the people, or who help distribute the sacrament, those who lead the music, or welcome worshippers before or after the service: all are ministers at the service. Each of us has our role to play, growing in understanding of God's word and his gifts, growing in the care and devotion with which we prepare for and take part in the service, and growing in love and fellowship with the eucharistic community, fed by the body and blood of Christ to minister to God's world.

5 Round the Seasons: the Christian Year

One of the glories of our northern climate is the steady passage of the seasons: as winter draws to an end we long for spring; we rejoice in the long warm days of summer but the extended darkness of winter evenings provides an appropriate setting for the celebration of the mystery of Christmas. And so the passage of time marks itself, and we mark it too.

For people of faith, the annual passage of time reflects our awareness of God's bounty. The calendar of our Jewish ancestors in faith was closely related to their agricultural cycle, the festivals falling at significant moments. We can see a not dissimilar pattern in the agricultural calendars of the months that we find carved in wood or stone or painted in frescoes or on glass in some mediaeval churches. The Christian calendar derives in part from each of these calendars and helps us recall and celebrate the significant events of our Lord's life within the context of the annual cycle of the seasons. Indeed, the Latin word *Temporale*, which describes the ordering of the cycle of the main festivals and Sundays of the year, implies the ordering of time. The other cycle of the calendar, the *Sanctorale*, refers to the organization of saints' days throughout the year.

The Christian calendar inherited the seven day week from Judaism. The fourth commandment is: 'Six days you shall labour and do all your work, but the seventh day is a Sabbath to the Lord your God' (Exodus 20:9). As the Church spread through the Gentile world, the observance of the Sabbath on the seventh day gave way to the custom of keeping Sunday, the day of Jesus's resurrection and the first day of the week, as the principal day for worship together.

Seasons

Easter was at first the only annual Christian festival and marked the death and resurrection of Jesus on a single day, coinciding with the Jewish Passover. Gradually the celebration was lengthened and came to a conclusion on the fiftieth day by celebrating the gift of the Holy Spirit, described in Acts 2, coinciding with the Jewish feast of Pentecost. It also became the custom for Christians in Jerusalem to recall the events of Jesus's passion in the week preceding Easter. Pilgrims who visited Jerusalem for this solemnity took this custom away with them, sharing it at home and developing in local churches dramatic re-enactments of the passion and the events leading up to it. Thus the pattern of celebrating Holy Week and Easter with which we are familiar today emerged. In addition there developed the custom of commemorating Christ's forty days in the wilderness with a forty-day fast preceding Easter: this is the origin of Lent. It was especially a time of preparation for baptism, the favoured time for which was Easter, and also a time of public penance for people who had committed serious sins.

The origins of the other significant season – Advent, Christmas and Epiphany – are less easy to determine. It used to be considered that their midwinter location was intended as a means of sanctifying earlier pagan midwinter festivities, but it has also been argued that the date is a result of calculations to determine the date of Jesus's birth from the date of his death. Again originally there was one significant day, celebrating together the birth of Jesus and the visit of the wise men, kept on 25 December in the West and 6 January in the East. In time both dates came to celebrated, each with its own particular focus. The season of Advent emerged around the four Sundays preceding Christmas, as a time of preparation for the coming of the Messiah, the two earlier Sundays focused on the second coming and the final two Sundays on the announcement of the Messiah.

In this way, with a short break, we find almost half the year devoted to two distinctly focused episodes of remembrance and celebration related to the earthly life of Christ, beginning with a season of preparation for his coming marked by the First Sunday of Advent. The second part of the year, from Pentecost to Advent is less intensive, though it gathers momentum towards the end with All Saints' Day and All Souls' Day on 1 and 2 November, and ending with the celebration of the kingship of Christ on the Sunday before Advent.

Saints

The Calendar as we have it in *Common Worship* is, of course, the result of many changes and adaptations since the principal feasts, described above, emerged between the second and fifth centuries after Christ's birth. On the eve of the Reformation the calendar contained a host of saints' days and festivals. In England, the *Book of Common Prayer* abolished many of them as a simplification. For the many largely illiterate rural communities who had come to rely on the customs associated with the keeping of saints' days to mark time, this must have been confusing. However, the changes in the calendar in the *Book of Common Prayer* as it finally emerged were rather less drastic than those in many of the other Churches influenced by the Reformation. Liturgical changes during the twentieth century, in many denominations, have seen enormous enrichment of the calendar. This has included the reintroduction of some pre-Reformation feasts, and the commemoration of the lives and contributions of significant Christian figures of more recent times and from many nations and cultures. There has also been a renewed observance of significant seasonal observations such as Mothering Sunday and harvest festival.

The calendar is visible in churches through the use of significant colours for hangings and for the vestments of the clergy. The use of liturgical colours seems to have begun in the twelfth century and was preserved to only a limited extent by the Church of England at the Reformation. However, during the twentieth century there was a developing understanding of the importance of visual and physical, as well as spoken, expressions of worship, and liturgical colour schemes have been embraced by Christians of diverse traditions.

6 Glory to God: the Gloria in Excelsis

The Gloria is a hymn of praise and its name derives from its opening words in Latin, *Gloria in excelsis Deo*: 'Glory to God in the highest'. It was used first as a hymn at morning prayers and then in the fifth century it came to be sung at the beginning of the Eucharist, at first only at festivals. Its place as a song of praise in the Eucharist is unique to the western Church and it was originally restricted to celebrations at which the bishop was present. A later development allowed it on Easter night to mark the proclamation of the Resurrection, and in some places today there is still a tradition of ringing bells as the first Gloria of Easter is sung. By the eleventh century the use of the Gloria at the beginning of Sunday celebrations, other than in Advent and Lent, became the norm. This is how it is used today. In the 1662 *Book of Common Prayer*, the Gloria was placed at the end of the service of Holy Communion, perhaps as a climactic expression of praise. More recent forms of service have moved it back to its ancient place near the beginning of the service, and in placing it during the *Gathering*, *Common Worship* follows this pattern.

The Gloria falls into three sections.

The first is inspired by the words of the angels' song to the shepherds on the night of Jesus's birth, as it is recorded in the opening of the gospel according to Luke (Luke 2:14).

The second section expresses adoration, praising God the Father, as almighty, lord and heavenly king.

The third section is addressed to Christ, in his distinctive role as the one who takes away our sins and prays for us. John the Baptist identified Jesus at the beginning of his ministry as the Lamb of God who takes away the sin of the world (John 1:29), a role linked to the lambs sacrificed at Passover (see Chapter 11 *Remembrance and Sacrifice: the Eucharistic Prayer*, page 145). The title is also found in the Book of Revelation where the writer describes his vision of the Lamb in Glory (Revelation 5, 6, 21, 22). We ask Jesus to have mercy on us and to receive our prayers and conclude with an affirmation of Jesus's power as Holy One and Lord, a member of the Trinity.

7 Praying Together: the Collect

The collect, and its very close relation, the post communion prayer, trace their form back to the practice of the Church in Rome as early as the fifth century. A number of the collects found in *Common Worship* are faithful translations of prayers that have been in the western Christian tradition for many centuries.

Collects have a distinctive form, and knowing something about their pattern of construction is helpful when we come to use them devotionally. Although there are exceptions, a collect generally has five standard steps:

- An address to God the Father. Sometimes, especially in places where it was important to defend the divine nature of Jesus Christ, some collects were addressed to the Son.

- A clause or statement emphasising a particular attribute of God. This forms the basis for the following petition, although a few collects do not contain a petition.

- The petition, which is usually a single request on behalf of the whole Church, or for those present at worship.

- A statement of the purpose of the petition.

- A conclusion that asks for the mediation of Jesus, offering our prayer to the Father.

The function of the collect is to sum up the Gathering, or ritual of entrance, greeting and preparation at the opening of the Eucharist. In other words, it gathers or 'collects' the petitions of the clergy and people in a focused intention expressed in a single prayer. This does not, however, rule out the importance of scriptural reference in the composition of collects. Especially during seasons such as Easter or Advent, there is often a close link between the day's Bible readings and the themes of the collect. The First Sunday of Advent is a very good example of this association.

Each Sunday of the Church year (see Chapter 5 Round the Seasons: the Christian Year, page 132) has an appointed collect. In addition, individual collects are provided for holy days, and there are common collects for other commemorations. Common Worship preserves a number of collects that are found in the Book of Common Prayer, some of them with origins in much earlier service books of the ancient Church in Rome. It has also kept some collects from the Alternative Service Book, and there are some new compositions.

Common Worship also provides a post communion prayer. Similar in form to the collect, there is one for each Sunday and holy day, with common prayers for other commemorations. They are a clear, simple thanksgiving for communion together with a petition that usually looks to the coming of the kingdom of God. We are reminded, as we celebrate at God's table on earth, that we are called ultimately to his banquet in heaven.

8 Listening to the Word: the Lectionary

The tradition of reading Scripture is one of the earliest features of Christian worship and derives from the Jewish practice of reading the Torah and the psalms within the context of worship. The very earliest Christian communities would have continued to read the Jewish scriptures, and this would be followed by comment. The letters written by Paul and others were perhaps originally read at this point as a Christian commentary on the reading. The practice of reading from these letters (or 'epistles') may derive from this. The telling of stories about Jesus's life, which became the gospels, followed.

By the fifth century the custom of reading particular passages of scripture for particular feasts had developed. At Easter there were readings about the resurrection and, in the days that followed, stories from the Acts of the Apostles about the beginning of the Church. Eventually a pattern of three readings, prescribed for certain Sundays of the year, emerged, together with the custom of singing a psalm after the Old Testament reading and as a commentary upon it.

For many centuries this pattern was lost, but it was revived in the 1960s and is followed by the Sunday lectionary (or cycle of readings) in Common Worship. There are three readings and a psalm for the 'Principal Service' each week, and for other holy days. The readings provided are from an international, ecumenical scheme known as the 'Revised Common Lectionary', and this has been adapted in minor ways to meet the needs of the Church of England at this time.

Reading the Gospels

The lectionary is based on a three-year cycle which focuses on one of the 'synoptic Gospels' (Matthew, Mark and Luke) each year, designated Years A, B and C, respectively. Readings from the gospel according to John supplement this, particularly on the Sundays of Easter and Epiphany. Readings from John also supplement provision in Year B, when the gospel readings are mainly from Mark, the shortest of the gospels. In this way it is possible, over time, for us to develop a sense of the distinctive-ness of each of the gospels and to hear a considerable portion read. Indeed, over the course of the three-year cycle, in the three readings and the psalm, a large proportion of the Bible is read aloud to regular worshippers.

Reading the Old and New Testaments

Outside the seasonal provision (Advent and Christmas, Lent and Easter) the lectionary provides two different schemes for reading the Old Testament. One aims to provide an Old Testament reading which complements the Gospel reading. In the other, specific Old Testament books are read over a number of consecutive Sundays, providing a sense of the continuity of the Old Testament narrative. Other New Testament readings (the second reading) are also read in a more continuous fashion. Readings from the Acts of Apostles, used instead of the Old Testament reading in Eastertide, remind us of the custom of the ancient Christian communities described above. The use of a psalm after the Old Testament reading is particularly encouraged and provides an opportunity for us to regain a familiarity with the psalter. The psalms may be said or sung: a variety of musical settings in a range of styles, new and old, is available, making it easier for the whole congregation to participate in this part of the service.

When there is more than one service in a church on a Sunday or holy day, *Common Worship* provides other cycles of readings which complement those read at the Principal Service, so that even more of the Bible is heard.

Closed and Open Seasons

Another noteworthy feature of the cycle of Sunday readings provided in *Common Worship* is the idea of a 'closed' season and an 'open' season. The 'closed' season is from the First Sunday of Advent to the Presentation of Christ in the Temple and from Ash Wednesday to Trinity Sunday. In these periods, the readings are chosen very specifically to the needs of the season, and they should be used as set in the lectionary with no variation. However, during the 'open' season, more flexibility is available, so that worship leaders and teachers within a congregation may, if it is fitting, explore a particular book of the Bible, or teaching theme, in more depth than would be possible by a straight use of the lectionary provision.

Preaching a Sermon

The readings from the Bible are normally followed by a sermon. Like the readings, this is an integral part of the proclamation of the Word of God. It may be a formal exposition of the biblical texts but it may on some occasions be appropriate to use a less formal teaching and learning style, encouraging members of the congregation to engage with the texts in a variety of interactive or reflective ways. Sometimes it will be appropriate to divide into age or interest groups and on other occasions, it may be helpful to encourage a decidedly intergenerational engagement with the Bible.

9 We Believe: the Nicene Creed

In the words of the creed we declare our acceptance of the Christian faith as it has been stated by the Church down the ages. It is a corporate statement, rather than a statement of personal belief: this is what the Church teaches, and this is what we collectively believe as members of the Church. But creeds have had, and still have, different significances at different times and places.

The word 'creed' comes from the Latin *credo*, meaning 'I believe', and for many centuries, although not originally, the words 'I believe' were used in the creed. The translation used in *Common Worship* recovers the original 'We believe'.

Creeds originated as baptismal affirmations. They set out the key elements of the Christian doctrine, and candidates for baptism were expected to repeat them as a public declaration of their allegiance to the faith they were embracing. Baptismal preparation included instruction in this and other formulas. The creed called the Apostles' Creed (see page 101) began in this way, and it is still used in the baptism service.

From the second and third centuries, Christian teachers needed to proclaim the faith among sophisticated philosophers, particularly in the great intellectual centres at such cities as Alexandria and Antioch in the Greek-speaking east of the Roman Empire. They had to use language with which they could converse with other philosophers and scholars, especially the more abstract language used by the Greek intellectuals. The teachings of Jesus were related in the gospels, but these contain little detail about the nature of the Messiah and his relationship with the God of the Old Testament. These were the subject of intense philosophical and theological debate.

Nicaea and After

Early in the fourth century the Roman Emperor, Constantine, gave his approval to Christianity. There was a debate on the nature of Christ between two views: those who ranked Christ lower than God (called Arians, after the leading proponent of this view, Arius) and those who proclaimed Christ as fully divine. Constantine summoned a great council of bishops, mostly from the eastern part of the Roman Empire, as well as some from the west, to resolve this dispute. They met at Nicaea, in what is now Turkey, in the year 325.

The Council almost unanimously agreed a formula affirming that Christ was of one substance (or 'of one Being') with the Father. Not all of those in support understood this statement in precisely the same way, however, nor was it precisely the form of words which we now call the Nicene Creed. It had little to say about the Holy Spirit or the Church.

In 381, another council of bishops met in Constantinople, and it is the creed associated with this council that has survived as the Nicene Creed. This creed made a firm statement about the relationship of Father, Son and Holy Spirit within the unity of the Trinity.

This was not the end of controversy, and later councils needed to reiterate the Church's teaching on the human and divine nature of Christ, and to affirm their agreement with the creed of the Council of Constantinople.

An Addition to the Creed

The creed was intended as a statement of orthodox belief. Over the years various views were put forward which were regarded as heretical, and sometimes words or phrases were locally added to the creed to combat them. One such addition has proved to be controversial: the words 'and the Son' added to the creed in the phrase about the Holy Spirit 'who proceeds from the Father and the Son'. These words, often known by the Latin translation filioque, were inserted by a Spanish council in 589, and gradually came into use across the western, Latin-speaking, Church. The eastern Churches never agreed to the inclusion of the filioque in the creed, and it remains one of the grounds for the division of eastern and western Christendom. Common Worship contains (on page 140) a version of the creed which does not include the phrase. This version is for use 'on suitable ecumenical occasions'.

Over time the creed came to be said regularly at the Eucharist by all the faithful: at first perhaps a few times a year, and eventually week by week. In the Book of Common Prayer it is recited at every celebration of Holy Communion. In recent revisions of the Eucharist it is optional, though it should be used on Sundays and important holy days.

We Believe

The Nicene Creed states our belief in God who is the creator of all things. Following the example of the early councils, it opens with the words 'We believe'. This makes it clear that the creed is a profession of orthodoxy by a body of believers, not by a single individual.

The section about the Son is perhaps the most complex, with difficult theological language. It affirms that Christ is 'eternally begotten of the Father'. The Son exists eternally with the Father; he is not a subsequent creation, although the relation between these two persons of the Trinity is usefully described in terms of the relationship of Son to Father. It affirms that everything was created through God the Son, as the first chapter of the gospel according to John proclaims. And it affirms that the Son, through whom all things were created, became, at a particular moment in history, a human being like us. Like us, he lived and died, but he rose from that death to be at the right hand of God the Father.

The creed goes on to affirm belief in God the Holy Spirit, who is one with the Father and the Son, and whose inspiration is behind the words of the prophets of the Old Testament and the New. It then makes a statement about the Church: that it is 'one' and 'holy'; 'catholic', that is, universal; and 'apostolic', that is, founded by the first followers of Jesus and commissioned to spread the gospel to all people. It states our belief in baptism as the sacrament that washes away our sins and provides the gateway to membership of the Church. It proclaims the Church's belief in the resurrection, and in the promise of eternal life.

The creed, then, is an historical document from a defining period in the Church's history. By affirming our faith in its words, we stand with Christians down the centuries and across the world who have done the same. This is what 'We believe'.

10 Thanks and Praise: the Eucharistic Prayer

At the heart of the Eucharist is the *Liturgy of the Sacrament*. In this section of the service the bread and wine are taken and then blessed, the bread is broken, and the bread and wine are shared. The eucharistic prayer is the second of these four actions, the prayer of blessing and thanksgiving, in which these ordinary everyday foods become for us the body and blood of Christ to be shared in communion. The word 'eucharist' means 'giving thanks' in Greek, and both this prayer and the service are named after this theme which is so central.

History

We know little about the very early forms of the eucharistic prayer. Paul recalls (in 1 Corinthians 11:23–25) the tradition that was handed on to him. Justin, martyred at Rome around 165, writes that the bread and cup were brought to the president who led the prayer of thanksgiving. These prayers may have derived from the Jewish prayers of blessing which preceded a meal, and the prayer over the cup after the meal, but we do not know what form this took, or even if there was a single prayer or several. From a little later, we have the prayer, usually attributed to Hippolytus of Rome in the early third century, which is given as an example of a eucharistic prayer. This is a single prayer and it contains several of the features which have come to be regarded as essential in a eucharistic prayer.

Shape

In Order One of the Eucharist in *Common Worship* there are eight different eucharistic prayers. They provide a variety of ways of giving thanks, with different styles and lengths, and different amounts of congregational participation. Some of them are derived from traditional or ancient prayers, some are modern and ecumenical, others are specific to *Common Worship*. This variety expresses some of the depths of meaning which lie in the Eucharist, and allows different emphases to be made. In many churches, different prayers will be used at different times through the year, and this enables the congregation to experience this variety as well as coming to know each prayer through sustained use. But the prayers all have various features in common, and just as there is a simple structure to the Eucharist (see Chapter 2 *Structure, Variety: the Shape of the Eucharist*, page 123), so there is a simple structure common to the eucharistic prayers.

There are several ways of looking at the shape of the prayers. First, they are *trinitarian*: each begins by praising God the Father, moves on to recall the life on earth of Jesus Christ, God the Son, and then prays for the gift of God the Holy Spirit. This shape reminds us of the Christian understanding of God as Three in One: Creator, Redeemer and Sanctifier.

Secondly, each prayer is divided between *praise* and *petition*. The prayer always opens with a dialogue in which we say that it is right to give thanks and to praise God, and we do this by proclaiming the 'mighty acts' of God. This may be by summarizing the history of the revelation of God as recorded in the Old and New Testaments, or, especially on festivals, it may be by focusing on one particular aspect of that revelation. Each prayer then continues by making petitions or requests to God. These requests are for the benefits of the sacrament: that we may receive the body and blood of Christ; that receiving the sacrament we may be drawn closer to the kingdom of God; that the faithful may all be gathered together in that kingdom; and so on. The items which form part of these *praise* and *petition* sections vary between the prayers, as we shall see.

Thirdly, each prayer contains several elements that have become traditional, or even essential, in a eucharistic prayer. Even at first glance it is obvious that the prayers all begin with the same dialogue between the president and the congregation, each contains the congregational 'Holy, holy, holy' (the *Sanctus*) and each recalls the words and actions of Jesus at the Last Supper. But the prayers have more in common than this and all are composed of the following elements:

- An opening greeting and dialogue.

- The *preface*: an opening section of praise which may be very brief, and may be supplemented or replaced with a special text appropriate to the occasion (this is called a *proper preface*). In all except Prayer H this leads into...

- The song 'Holy, holy, holy' (the *Sanctus*) which may be followed by 'Blessed is he' (the *Benedictus*).

- Some prayers now move from *praise* to *petition* with a brief request that the Holy Spirit may come down on the bread and wine. (This petition is called the *epiclesis*.) The other prayers remain in *praise*.

- The story of the Last Supper (the *institution narrative*).

- An explicit statement that we are following Christ's command to 'do this in remembrance of me' (this is the *anamnesis*). See Chapter 11 *Remembrance and Sacrifice: the Eucharistic Prayer*, page 145.

- A request for the gift of the Holy Spirit that we may receive all the benefits for which we pray. (This may include the *epiclesis* if that has not been prayed earlier, or it may be a prayer for 'worthy reception'.) There may be other requests, and this may be linked to the prayers of all the faithful, and may mention individual saints by name.

- A final section of praise, the *doxology*, leading to the congregational 'Amen'. In Prayer H this takes the form of the song 'Holy, holy, holy' (the *Sanctus*).

In *Come to the Feast*, the pages opposite the eucharistic prayers (pages 48–91) mark the start of each of these sections.

The prayers also differ in the words said by the congregation, and some of the prayers have optional responses for the congregation.

Contents

The above outline contains a number of technical words, and some of these are worth further explanation.

The *institution narrative* recites the story of the Last Supper at which Jesus took bread and wine, blessed them and shared them, with the command that his disciples should 'do this in remembrance of me'. Paul's first letter to the Corinthians (1 Corinthians 11:23–25) is the earliest written record we have of the Last Supper, and this has been the usual base of the narrative since the Reformation. Other traditions have at times included other scriptural and non-scriptural words as well. The narrative can be seen as simply telling the story of why we are celebrating, but it is at the same time part of the memorial, and one of the things for which we give thanks. It also has a particular significance which we shall consider shortly.

The *anamnesis* follows the institution narrative. The Greek word *anamnesis* is perhaps best translated as 'remembrance' or 'memorial', and its role is to point out that in this service, this Eucharist, this eucharistic prayer, we are obeying Christ's command. Over the years there has been much discussion over precisely what this remembrance means, with beliefs varying from a bloodless sacrifice repeating the death of Christ to a mere bringing to mind. Chapter 11 *Remembrance and Sacrifice: the Eucharistic Prayer*, page 145, looks at this question in greater detail.

Epiclesis is another Greek word, this time referring to the invocation of the Holy Spirit. In each of the eight prayers in Order One of *Common Worship* the epiclesis marks the start of the petitionary section of the prayer. But the prayers differ in that with some (A, B, C and E) there is a brief invocation of the Spirit *before* the institution narrative, in which each of these prayers asks the Father that, through the Spirit, the bread and wine may be for us the body and blood of the Son. In the other prayers (D, F, G and H), however, this invocation comes *after* both the narrative and the anamnesis, a pattern which is found more in the eastern church than in the west.

Why is there this difference in the position of the invocation of the Spirit and what is its significance?

The variety of shape reflects a complex history in which different parts of the prayer came to be regarded by different people as being the single most important moment of the prayer. There has been a frequently-held tradition in the west that the institution narrative itself, and especially the words spoken by Christ ('this is my body' and 'this is my blood') are the effective moments in the prayer. By contrast, the eastern Church has traditionally tended to view the invocation of the Spirit, after the institution narrative, as the crux of the prayer.

Recent thinking, across the churches, east and west, catholic and protestant, instead views the entire prayer, from the opening dialogue to the congregational 'Amen', as having a single theme of blessing God and praying for his blessing on his Church. 'Consecration' is by thanksgiving, and the whole prayer is one of thanksgiving. This consensus, though not universal, enables us to move on from the entrenched positions of the past. Led by the president, but prayed by the whole congregation, it makes the entire prayer a sustained plea to God, Father, Son and Holy Spirit, that we may live in his kingdom and feast at his banquet.

11 Remembrance and Sacrifice: the Eucharistic Prayer

'Do this in remembrance of me.' These words at the heart of the Eucharist remind us what we are doing. The first three gospels and Paul's first letter to the Corinthians record that Jesus, at the Last Supper, took bread and wine, gave thanks over them, and distributed them to his disciples, telling them to 'do this in remembrance of me'. The Church, as the successors of those disciples, continues this act.

Remembering the Past

But what is it that we are doing? What are we remembering and why?

The Last Supper took place at the time of Passover: in Matthew, Mark and Luke it is a Passover meal, whilst in John it is the day before Passover. Either way, it is the Jewish feast of the Passover which provided the context of the Last Supper. The story of the first Passover is recorded in Exodus 12: the Jewish people, trying to escape from Egypt, sacrificed lambs and daubed the blood on their doorposts. The angel of death visited Egypt, destroying the firstborn male of every house but passed over houses daubed in blood. In the ensuing uproar, the Jewish people made good their escape. In commemoration, they kept this feast every spring thereafter.

Later, a second festival was associated with this: the first fruits of the barley harvest were offered at the Temple in Jerusalem, and as part of this all yeast products were destroyed, and only unleavened bread eaten, so that afterwards the new bread could be made with new yeast.

By remembering the Passover each year, the Jewish people believe that they are entering into the original Passover and flight from Egypt. Each year the story of the first Passover is retold and they share in the escape from Pharaoh, the crossing of the Red Sea, the eating of manna from heaven, the crying of tears in the desert, but most importantly they share in the deliverance from the angel of death, which made possible their escape.

From the earliest times Christians have seen the death of Jesus as being the fulfilment of the Passover sacrifice – Paul writes that Christ is the Passover lamb sacrificed for us (1 Corinthians 5:7), and in the same way that each subsequent Passover is in remembrance of the first Passover, so the Eucharist is in remembrance of Christ's death on the cross. At the Eucharist, then, we remember the past. But also, in our collective memory, we make present that past event.

Making Present the Past

As those participating at the Passover have in remembrance the sacrifice of the lambs and the subsequent deliverance of their homes from the death of the firstborn, so Christ is the new Passover sacrifice by whose death we are saved from death. As the covenant between God and the Jewish people was sealed by the blood smeared on the doorways of their homes, and by the blood of subsequent sacrifices sprinkled over the people by Moses (Exodus 24:8–9), so the blood of Christ seals the new covenant of God with all people. As the first fruits of the barley harvest, symbolic of the new leavened bread, were offered at the Temple a few days after the Passover sacrifice, so a few days after Good Friday Christ is risen from the dead, the first-fruit of those who have died, risen to new life in which we share. As those who celebrate the Passover hold this act of remembrance to be a participation in, and a making present of, the original event, so by our remembrance of the words and deeds of Christ at the Last Supper we are similarly present at, and partakers of, the original event, and the sacrifice of Christ at Calvary, a once-only event, is made present for us in the Eucharist.

The sacrifice is also a 'sacrifice of praise and thanksgiving' in which we offer to God the duty and service that we owe. Faith is a living relationship with God, right here and now, and as we remember and make present the sacrifice of Calvary, so we are caught up in Christ's saving act, and are united with his body and blood, as suggested by 1 Corinthians 10:16 and John 6:51–58.

This, then, is what we mean by *anamnesis*, by remembrance, and it is in this remembrance that we pray that the bread and wine may be for us the body and blood of Christ. It is this that we affirm when we say 'Amen' at the end of the eucharistic prayer and again when we receive the sacrament.

The Presence of Christ

Christians have interpreted the presence of Christ in the Eucharist in a variety of ways. The presence of Christ is a sacramental presence: there is an outward and visible sign – the bread and the wine – which hides the inward and spiritual grace – the body and blood of Christ, and the forgiveness of sins which that brings. From the earliest times, Christians have denied that the Eucharist is a cannibalistic meal: some have held that in some way Christ is physically present under the appearance of bread and wine, and others have believed that the presence is in the hearts and minds of those who faithfully give thanks and eat and drink the bread and wine. Yet others have held positions between these. Anglicans have generally taken the view that the precise nature of the presence of Christ

is a mystery, a position summed up in words attributed to
both John Donne, Dean of St Paul's (1573–1631) and Queen
Elizabeth I (1533–1603):

> 'Twas God the Word that spake it,
> he took the Bread and brake it;
> And what the Word did make it,
> That I believe, and take it.

12   Our Father: the Lord's Prayer

'As our Saviour taught us, so we pray.' These or similar words
introduce the Lord's Prayer and remind us that the gospels
record how Jesus taught his disciples to pray. There are two
accounts, one in Luke 11:1–4, the other in Matthew 6:7–13.
In Luke's account, some of the disciples note that John the
Baptist had taught his disciples what to say when praying and
they asked Jesus to do the same. In Matthew the context is
slightly different, and Jesus makes a contrast between mere
outward show and real prayer. The two gospels have slightly
different forms of the prayer: Matthew's is the more familiar to
us, because the form used in worship has been based upon it;
Luke's is shorter and more abrupt. Perhaps Jesus taught
different forms on different occasions; or perhaps the same
occasion is recorded differently; perhaps the gospels represent
different summaries of Jesus's teaching. Or perhaps these two
forms were in liturgical use in the communities where the
gospels were written, so that each recorded the form familiar
from their own worship.

The prayer has a simple structure. It consists of an opening
address to God the Father, then four lines containing three
requests about God's kingdom. This is followed by further
requests, this time concerning us. Each can be looked at in
greater detail.

Our Father

The opening words, 'Our Father' tell us two things. First, it is
primarily a prayer to be said collectively: we do not say 'My
Father'. This wording ('us', 'our') continues in the second half
of the prayer. It reminds us that the teachings of Jesus can only
be fulfilled by working and worshipping with others.
Secondly, Jesus calls God 'Father'. We are so familiar with this
fact that it is hard to think of it as novel. The Old Testament

contains many references to God as the Father of his people, but Jesus moves beyond this, referring to God as we refer to our own fathers. In Aramaic, the word is *Abba*, used by Jesus elsewhere (for example, at Gethsemane, see Mark 14:36), which we might almost translate as 'Dad' or 'Daddy'. It is a sign of the close relationship which Jesus felt to God the Father. Now Jesus tells us to pray 'Our Father' in the same intimate way – a sign that we too have been adopted as the sons and daughters of God.

Hallowed Be Your Name

The next three lines have a similar grammatical structure in Greek, each line starting with a verb and ending with a noun. In English only the first ('hallowed be your name') follows this form, although the similarity can be maintained by saying:

may your name be hallowed,
may your kingdom come,
may your will be done…

Together they are a request that the divine order be made visible on earth as it is in heaven – to the praise and glory of God.

A name is intimately associated with what it names, and God's name came to be seen as too holy to be said. Most translations of the Old Testament follow this by replacing the name of God (the Hebrew letters YHWH – Yahweh or Jehovah) with the words 'the LORD'. To hallow something is to set it apart and recognise it as holy, and when we pray that God's name be hallowed, we are praying that everything about God be recognised as holy, by us and by the world.

Your Kingdom Come

The next lines are key to the prayer: we pray for the coming of the kingdom of God, God's rule on earth, where everything is done as he wills it. The proclamation that the kingdom of God is at hand is central to the teaching of Jesus. It begins his ministry (Matthew 4:17; Mark 1:15; Luke 4:43); it lies behind many of the parables ('the kingdom of God is like this…'); and it is particularly appropriate at the Eucharist, which is itself a foretaste of the banquet in the kingdom of God. But this is not just a request that God will make his kingdom come. It is also a request that we might help to bring about that kingdom, here and now.

Our Daily Bread

The prayer now switches, and we make three requests for ourselves. Each request comes in two parts, although this may not be immediately obvious in English. One word in the first presents some difficulty: the word translated as 'daily'. The Greek *epiousion* occurs nowhere else in the Bible or elsewhere except as a comment on this petition, so its meaning must be inferred from the context and from the word itself. There are several possible meanings: just enough to eat today; or the bread for tomorrow. And 'tomorrow' might mean the day after today, or it might mean the day when God's kingdom comes – the heavenly banquet itself, Jesus as the bread of life, and our anticipation of it in the sacramental bread of the Eucharist. We cannot be certain of the answer, but our praying can be enriched by these overlapping ideas.

Forgive Us

The second request is on the surface straightforward: 'Forgive us our sins'. Matthew has 'debts' and 'debtors', and forgiving a debt means writing it off, and that is what we ask God to do for us – but we must write off the debts and sins of others. Writing off someone else's sins is often hard, but so is writing off a debt. However, that is what Jesus teaches us to do.

Lead Us Not Into Temptation

The final request is also a difficult one in English. God does not lead us into temptation, and this might be better phrased 'Let us not be led into temptation'. The ecumenical version uses the translation 'Save us from the time of trial', and again the reference is to a peril or 'test' that may come: disowning Christ in the face of great danger or persecution, before the kingdom comes. We pray that we may be delivered from this evil, the work of the evil one.

Now And For Ever

The prayer ends with a sentence of praise (the *doxology*), added in 1662 under the influence of the 1611 Authorized Version of the Bible, which was derived from late mediaeval Greek manuscripts. More recent Bible translations are based on much older manuscripts and do not include it. However, these words, though non-biblical, are associated with the prayer from at least the fourth century, and make a fitting ending.

13 Go in Peace: the Dismissal

Once we have received the sacrament of communion, the
service moves quickly to an end. The Dismissal is a simple and
short final section. Perhaps notices will be given out, although
this might have happened before the service begins or before
the intercessions. There may be a hymn, and usually the president will pray God to bless the congregation. All of this is
optional. The only part which is mandatory is the dismissal
itself, 'Go in peace to love and serve the Lord,' or 'Go in the
peace of Christ'. And then we all leave.

Frequently this leaving is a ceremonial event. The ministers, and perhaps a choir, may process out of the church to a
vestry. The congregation may kneel and say a few words of
silent prayer, before getting up to leave. Perhaps an organist or
a music group will play – covering the hustle and bustle of
those departing.

That's it, then. We have 'been to church'. Now we can go
home, perhaps cook and eat the Sunday lunch, or go out for
the day, or otherwise relax and enjoy ourselves. Or after an
early morning weekday service we might speed off to work or
to the business of the day. If we are not careful then we can
quickly forget what we have been doing.

Fed by the Sacrament

In the sacrament of communion we have shared a foretaste of
the banquet in God's kingdom, a glimpse of God. The sacrament nourishes us, strengthening us in our task, and building
up our common life. It refreshes us for our everyday lives, for
the routine of work, school or home, and the ups and downs
of family life, career and health.

We have received the sacrament, and in the prayers that
follow we have asked God to strengthen us with the Spirit for
our work in the world. What is this work? It is the work that
we have heard and prayed about throughout the service: in the
proclamation of the Word in the readings and the sermon, in
the petitions of the eucharistic prayer, in the prayers after
communion, and most succinctly of all in the Lord's Prayer.
There we prayed to God 'your kingdom come'. Our work, our
mission, is to help bring about now that kingdom, that reign
of God, on earth as in heaven. However great this task, and
however small our role, each of us has a part to play.

Christianity is an 'incarnational' religion: God became a human being as Jesus of Nazareth. He got his hands dirty, living as a carpenter in a Middle Eastern town. He knew what it was like to be a child, to have fun and to cry, to grow up and earn a living, to have friends and to be alone, to party and to mourn, to be healthy and to be ill, to be mocked, to suffer and to die. He spent several years proclaiming to people that the kingdom of God was at hand, if only they had eyes to see and ears to hear.

In the Eucharist we proclaim that now we are the body of Christ. Teresa of Avila (1515–82) put this forcefully when she wrote:

> Christ has no body now but yours,
> No hands, no feet on earth but yours,
> Yours are the eyes with which he looks out with compassion on this world.
> Yours are the feet with which he walks to do good.
> Yours are the arms with which he blesses all the world.
> Yours are the hands, yours are the feet, you are his eyes, you are his body.
> Christ has no body now on earth, but yours.

The words of the second congregational prayer after communion also remind us that we are now Christ's body and we share his risen life. We drink his cup, remembering what he said to the disciples James and John, that this cup may be a share in his suffering (see Matthew 20:20–23; Mark 10:35–40). It may be difficult, but through this cup we must present the life of the risen Christ to other people. The Spirit lights us, and we are to shine as lights in the world. How are we to do this?

This is Our Story, This is Our Song

We must tell the story of God: that he cares about the world we live in and about each one of us. We must proclaim the good news of Jesus in each generation. This is our story: the story of Jesus's life and teaching; the story of his death and resurrection. And this is our song: Jesus is alive in us and with us now.

The kingdom of God, Jesus proclaimed, is at hand: good news to the poor, release to captives, sight to the blind, freedom to the oppressed (Isaiah 61:1–2; Luke 4:16–21). This vision of God's kingdom is continued in the Beatitudes (Matthew 5:1–11; Luke 6:20–22) and in parables such as Matthew 25:31–46, especially verses 37–40.

We must make the connection between what we do in church and what we do in our lives, and we must do it in a way that helps others to make that connection too. As we do this, we are living witnesses in the world to the reality of God, and we have a foretaste of God's reign.

At the end of the gospel according to Matthew, the disciples receive the great commission from Christ: they are to go and make disciples of all nations. And that is our task, the task for which we are sent out into the world.

Go in peace to love and serve the Lord.
In the name of Christ. Amen.

Further Reading

In a book of this size it is only possible to begin to touch
upon many aspects of the Eucharist and of the Christian faith.
The books listed here will enable you to explore further many
of the themes of this book. There are many more books on the
subject and several of those listed below have comprehensive
suggestions for further study.

Using Common Worship: Holy Communion
Mark Beach
Church House Publishing, 2000

> A practical guide to the Common Worship services of Holy
> Communion with imaginative suggestions for use in various
> local situations.

Companion to Common Worship, Volume 1
Paul Bradshaw (ed.)
SPCK, 2001

> An historical survey and detailed commentary for each of
> the services in Common Worship: Services and Prayers for the Church
> of England.

Living the Eucharist
Stephen Conway (ed.)
Darton, Longman and Todd, 2001

> A collection based on papers given at a conference,
> organized by Affirming Catholicism, in the form of an extended
> Eucharist celebrated and explored over four days.

Common Worship Today
Mark Earey and Gilly Myers (eds)
HarperCollins, 2001

> An attractive, large-format, full-colour introduction to all
> the Common Worship services, this book features an extensive
> and readable section on the Eucharist.

Our Thanks and Praise
David Holeton (ed.)
Anglican Book Centre, Toronto, 1998

> Comprising papers from an international gathering of
> Anglican liturgical scholars in 1995, this book describes the

historical, liturgical and theological background for the revision of the Eucharist in many parts of the Anglican Communion. Although not for the faint-hearted, it will repay those who have the time for its far-reaching study.

Mass Culture: eucharist and mission in a post-modern world
Pete Ward (ed.)
Bible Reading Fellowship, Oxford, 1999
  Seven contributors 'examine the impact of the Eucharist on believers and outsiders today'.

http://www.oremus.org/come-to-the-feast
  An on-line companion to *Come to the Feast*, featuring a further reading list and other useful information.

Glossary

absolution

After the confession, the president prays that God will forgive us our sins. This is the absolution. See page 21.

agnus dei

The anthem 'Lamb of God' sung during the breaking of the bread.

anamnesis

A Greek word meaning 'remembrance', the act of making present a past event; also a sentence in the eucharistic prayer in which we explicitly link what we are doing with Christ's command to 'do this in remembrance of me'.

deacon

A member of the threefold ministry of bishops, priests and deacons. A deacon has a traditional role at the Eucharist, complementary to that of the president. The deacon may read the gospel, and invite or lead the responses of the people in the service. See page 158 of *Common Worship: Services and Prayers for the Church of England*.

doxology

A short hymn of praise to God. The eucharistic prayers each end with a doxology, as does the Lord's Prayer.

epiclesis

A Greek word referring to the invocation of the Holy Spirit. In the eucharistic prayer we pray through the Spirit that the bread and wine may be for us the body and blood of Christ, and that as we receive the sacrament we may also receive all its benefits.

eschatology, eschatological

To do with the 'last things', such as the return of Christ, and particularly the coming of God's kingdom.

eucharist

A Greek word meaning 'thanksgiving'. It refers to the thanks we give in the service during the eucharistic prayer.

eucharistic prayer

The prayer at the heart of the service in which we give thanks for God's goodness, remembering all that he has done for our salvation, especially in the life, death and resurrection of Jesus Christ, and praying for the gift of the

Holy Spirit. In this prayer of thanksgiving the bread and wine become for us the body and blood of Christ, to be shared in the sacrament of communion.

filioque

A Latin word (pronounced 'fee-lee-o-kway') meaning 'and the Son'. It refers to the controversial addition of these words to the Nicene Creed.

institution narrative

A section of the eucharistic prayer in which the story of the Last Supper is told, at which Jesus instituted the Eucharist by his words and deeds.

passover

The principal festival of the Jewish year, commemorating the escape from Egypt recorded in the book of Exodus. The Last Supper took place at the time of Passover, and the idea of *anamnesis* derives from the way in which the Jews celebrate Passover.

preface

The first part of the eucharistic prayer, up to the *Sanctus*, in which we praise God, usually by reciting some of the mighty things he has done for his people.

president

The president presides over the service, saying the opening greeting, and leading many of the prayers including the collect and the eucharistic prayer. As the representative of the Church, the president pronounces the blessing and the absolution for our sins. The president must be a priest, ordained by the bishop, thus uniting us with congregations across the world and down the ages.

proper preface

Part of the preface in the eucharistic prayer, which is proper to a particular day or season. It may be added to the standard preface or may entirely replace it.

sacrament

One of the sacred ceremonies of the Church, especially Baptism and the Eucharist. A sacrament is the outward and visible sign of an inward and spiritual grace. At the Eucharist, the outward sign is the bread and wine; the spiritual grace is the body and blood of Christ, by which we receive forgiveness of our sins, union with Christ and one another, and a foretaste of the heavenly banquet.

Sanctus

The song of the angels, recorded in the vision of Isaiah (Isaiah 6:3). It was sung in the Temple at Jerusalem, and at an early stage became an integral part of the eucharistic prayer. In the Eucharist it is often followed by the *Benedictus*, the acclamation of the crowds who welcomed Jesus into Jerusalem on the first Palm Sunday.

Torah

The first five books of the Bible recording the revelation of God to Moses and enshrining the Jewish law. It contains 613 commandments, covering every area of daily life. The instructions are summed up most succinctly in the Ten Commandments.

Acknowledgments

The authors are grateful for permission to reproduce copyright material.

The Archbishops' Council, for permission to reproduce the text of Holy Communion Order One from *Common Worship: Services and Prayers for the Church of England* (Church House Publishing), copyright © The Archbishops' Council 2000, reproduced by permission. The selection of pages is from the separate *Holy Communion Order One* booklet.

The Rt Revd Andrew Burnham, Bishop of Ebbsfleet, for permission to reproduce, with two minor emendations, the Examination of Conscience on pages 112, 114 from *A Manual of Anglo-Catholic Devotion*, Canterbury Press Norwich, 2001, compilation copyright © Andrew Burnham 2001.

The quotation on page 126 is by Dom Gregory Dix (1901–1952) from *The Shape of the Liturgy*, Dacre, London, 1945, copyright Dom Gregory Dix 1945.

We also wish to thank:

Dr Bridget Nichols, who wrote early drafts of several chapters and contributed to the commentary pages;

Rachel Boulding, for her support for this book in its earliest stages, without which it would not have been written;

our friends and associates who took time to read the book in draft form and provide detailed criticism: the Revd Professor Paul Bradshaw, the Revd Gordon Giles, Robert Hudson, the Revd Alan Jesson, the Revd James Pullen, Brian Reid, Simon Sarmiento, the Rt Revd David Stancliffe, and Dr David Yeandle. Any remaining errors are, of course, our own.

Finally, we are grateful to our families – to Tom, and to Karen, Jennifer and Alexander – for their tolerance and their support during the writing of this book.